FAUSTO COPPI

The True Story

JEAN-PAUL OLLIVIER

FAUSTO COPPI
The True Story

Translated and revised by
Richard Yates

Charlie Woods
Stephanie Sanchez
with
Richard Allchin

Edited by
Richard Allchin

Sport and Publicity
For Bromley Books

Original French Version Published by Éditions de l'Aurore
6 Rue Lt Chananon BP177 38008 Grenoble France

This first English language Edition published by
Sport and Publicity,
Flat 2 75 Fitzjohns Ave Hampstead London NW3 6PD

for

Bromley Books,
11 The Terrace Barnes London SW13 0NP

Bromley Books is a division of
Bromley Television International Ltd

Original French Version Published by
Éditions de l'Aurore 6 Rue Lt Chananon BP
177 38008 Grenoble France
Photos: Agency Press Sports

Printed and bound in Britain by BPC, Dunstable.

A catalogue record for this book is available from the British Library.

ISBN: 0-953-139-506

Acknowledgments

The English edition of 'Fausto Coppi, The True Story' was born from the fact that a book on the 'Campionissimo' telling the remarkable full account of his life hadn't been made available before in the English lanaguage.

Although there had been booklets, and a short but entertaining hardback by the late Peter Duker - all of which are no longer available - none of these, we felt did the life of the 'Campionissimo' justice, no matter with how much love and passion they were written.

It was because of this that we asked Paris based cycling historian Richard Yates, to search out a book that he considered to be worthy of an English translation. This book is a result of that request.

Jean-Paul Ollivier, the author, is a household name in cycling mad France. He is a renowned figure in the world of cycle journalism and a former top television commentator with France 2 & 3, their two public channels. Many years after his original book on Fausto Coppi was published, he returned to Italy to do even more research and to bring the book up to date.

Why you may ask was a Frenchman's book on an Italian cycle racing champion chosen over an Italian publication?

The answer is simple; we are more likely to get a truly objective account by a less partisan journalist and we hope readers will find this to be the case.

We know that Coppi wasn't perfect in the way he conducted his himself. But he was clearly a very good man, and more to the point he was his own man. However, the word perfection can be applied to Coppi's life while he was riding his bike at the height of his powers. The phrase 'poetry in motion' could have been written just for him - he was simply that good.

Many people have helped with this book. Our thanks go to Richard Yates in particular, but also to Charlie Woods and to Stephanie Sanchez for helping with the English translation and whose advice was invaluable.

Other people have also been of great assistance; They include Charles Allan, Elizabeth Ayres, Phil Liggett, Roger St Pierre, David Reed, Tim Hilton, Vincenne Buonpane, Jess Polakoff, Mick Clark and not least David Duffield for making sure viewers to Eurosport never forget the name of Fausto Coppi. But the biggest thanks of all goes to the author, Jean Paul Ollivier, for writing such a magnificent account of Coppi's remarkable life.

Richard Allchin, Sport & Publicity

ADVENTURES IN THE PIEDMONT HILLS

"YOU ARE GOING TO MAKE UP YOUR MIND AND MARRY HER!"

Angelo-Teodoro Coppi's voice became suddenly harder, huskier, final, in fact...

This time Domenico didn't dare to confront 'the father'. He didn't even try to dodge the cutting request which in reality was more of an order. Now he cannot delay his decision any longer.

Angelo had seen enough of his son woo the girls on one hill then on another one. He is big, handsome, has a smooth and thin moustache which turns the girls heads. Until then his father had said little because his son's strong arms had helped so much with the work on the farm. He is diligent, never afraid to buckle down to his chores, until the Sunday of each week when he escapes in search of good times to the villages of Paderna, Montale Celli, Costa Vescovato, Carezzano and Spineto Scrivia. There he parties and hangs around the bars. At the dances, the young girls point him out secretly dreaming that he is going to invite them to a dance. In this art, you just need to observe him to understand that few of his friends succeed in trying to outdo his boldness.

This way Domenico wins the hearts of the pretty girls of the surrounding area and enjoys the ritual. Moreover, as an impressive strong strapping 'manboy', he often leads them into youthful adventures of which they don't always appreciate the consequences until they surface from a barn's straw, stunned by a moment of passion.

After one such incident, one day, a certain girl goes a little too far. She is from Montale Celli, one of the hills above the land of Castellania. Her name is Angiolina Boveri. She doesn't appear to be quite beautiful but her sweet ways and the generous temper to which she gives free rein, earn her the consideration of the people in the village. Moreover, her family's links with Don Domenico Boveri, priest of the parish, give her a kind of privilege.

However she didn't listen to heaven when she let herself go to commit the 'sin' with Domenico Coppi in the hollow of the hill in

Father Domenico

Mother Angiolina

The Coppi children : Dina, Livio, Serse, Fausto (top right) and Maria

Montale, watched over only by the moon as a mute witness.

The month of January came. The birth of Jesus has just been celebrated with joy when the rumour of a future childbirth - not quite so innocent - has just started at the home of Giuseppe's and Vittoria Boveri. What is there to do? What is the priest going to say? Without delay, Angiolina has to point out the 'culprit'. From the hill in Montale Celli to the one in San Bagio-Castellania, there is not much more than 3km. More than once, covered by the cloak of disgrace, they will cover that distance and knock at the green and worm-eaten door of the Coppi's. Giuseppe and Angelo understand each other; the women too. Today's youngsters have neither the old fashioned principles or the virtue of their parents. That's the way generations go. Ah! if the two could marry, the sin would be fast erased and Don Boveri could carry on practising his religion without fears of those earthly blots which may harm his ministry.

But Domenico has to be convinced. He loves Angliolina, yes, he admits it, but maybe not enough to give up the rest of his life for her. There are other girls. However he has to make things right. A child - his child - is due. The more time goes by, the deadline gets closer and the pressure becomes more intense.

The young farmer finally accepts his responsibility. He ties his destiny to Angiolina's on the 29 July 1914, a few days before the Great War started. A party is organised in the meadow next to the bride's house - a tiny party, almost a secret one - and the young husband and wife come to live in Castellania in the house of the Coppi's.

Three months later Imelda-Vittoria-Maria was born. She will be known by her third name. She is such a beautiful baby finally, almost everybody ends up thinking that the 'sin' could have indeed been holy.

But life goes on. The young girls lost a devoted admirer; Angiolina found a good husband who will give her four more children: Livio, in 1916; Claudina, the next year; Fausto, in 1919; and Serse, in 1923.

Castellania - a village of six hundred souls - is at the bottom of a hill where the arid earth requires a lot of attention in proportion to the profit one can expect from it. The vine cannot grow vigorously because the sun spares itself and only allows the blooming of a skinny and 'lazy' grape. People have to use candles to provide light in their houses and water is often hard to come by.

In Angiolina's bedroom, on the ground floor of the house by via Umberto - the only side street of the place - Fausto was born, fourth child of the family. It is 5:00 pm on September 15, 1919. The sun shines brightly and the wind has swept the autumn's leaves in front of the door. The new-born hardly weighs more than four pounds. At first sight one is taken aback by his huge eyes.

Domenico works even harder in the fields. With a growing family to support his responsibility increases.

It is Maria who goes to get him. He is not very far from their home. She mumbles softly,

'Mummy has brought us a child'. Then Domenico takes his daughter by her hand and promptly returns to his home. Livio and Claudina - nicknamed Dina - are already around the cradle, clinging to the tulle curtain. 'Beautiful child, Giulina!' all the neighbours agree.

With which name is the newly born going to be baptised? Domenico wishes to call him Fausto like his younger brother; the 'mamma' prefers Angelo like the paternal grandfather. Because of the determination of his spouse, Domenico gives in. He is named Angelo-Fausto for the sake of the civil authorities. However the father will eventually have the final word and continues to call him Fausto. A few months later his tenacity triumphs. Angelo-Fausto will be simply called Fausto.

He rapidly has health problems. While growing up, his bones are weak as a result of vitamin deficiency as the quality of the food available is very poor. Yet Fausto seems none the worse and happily plays with the children of the same age as him, sometimes even winning a few liras at the 'morra'; a favourite game of the young in Italy.

The village teacher's name is Albina Tartara. She is being courted by Fausto's uncle, Giuseppe, and in 1932 they will eventually marry. Because of this, she watches over the homework of her future nephew. Albina is a luscious woman who likes to laugh and sing, feels a lot of affection for him, but he doesn't return it. The homework and the lessons don't inspire him. He prefers to get the bicycle off the nail where it is hanging in the barn and ride to San Andrea, San Allogio or to Paderna. Despite the frame being too big for him, and bad paint work he enjoys riding even if he has difficulty reaching the pedals.

He later tells famous French journalist Rene de Latour 'I think the bicycle was abandoned in a dark corner, it hardly worked and of course nobody wanted to use it. It was very difficult to get it working as I didn't even have the money to buy a pair of brake blocks!'

However, Fausto can climb the hills breaking away alone from his young friends. But on the flat roads, his position on his machine gives him a dreadful pain in the calves.

One day - the 17th of October 1927 - Albina notes the absence of her pupil. The class is about to start. She opens her green register, and draws in a beautiful slanted script the letter 'P' in front of the name of the present pupils, then the nib hesitates an instant in front of the name of the pupil Angelo-Fausto Coppi and writes a light, light 'A'. 'A' as for absent. That day Domenico's son didn't appear at the lessons. What has happened to him?

On the 17th of October the morning is beautiful and all Fausto wants to do is ride his bike.

The next day Albina tackles young Fausto. 'You didn't come to school yesterday' Says the teacher angrily. 'Were you sick?'

'No, I was fine, I felt very good, miss', he answered cheekily. 'I rode my bicycle all morning. I beat the Chiappinis of San Andrea. I can ride well!' Albina doesn't appreciate his enthusiasm for his cycling talents or his continued cheek.

'Go to your seat and write one hundred times: I ought to be at school, not riding my bicycle.'

Fausto accomplishes his punishment with his head bowed humbly.

People often find the young Fausto taciturn and sullen. He doesn't like the games the children of his age plays and prefers the solitude of the fields. But eventually he opens up more. His little brother Serse was born in 1923 and looks strikingly like his elder brother. He is the fifth and last born of the family and Fausto looks after him in a very protective manner. He even tries very hard to get him admitted to school before the required age.

'Either he is coming with me to school or I won't go!' Fausto insists.

During these times Domenico keeps working very hard on the farm, moaning in harsh Piedmont dialect about the poverty of these tough times.

When he reaches twelve years old, Fausto comes to help when the school day finishes.

He will always have a special place in his heart for their little farm, for the barn which doesn't even have a proper door, where all the farming equipment was piled up. He loved the serenity of the countryside as a child and these feelings wouldn't desert him in the years to come.

But at thirteen he is going to leave. What has happened inside him? No one knows.

One evening, father and son are together working in the fields. The bells of the church on the hill of San Biagio have not yet rung. The evening sun has apparently decided to linger. Fausto suddenly heaves a long sigh and with a determined and definitive gesture drives his shovel in the tough ground of Piedmont.

Turning round toward his father and looking at him straight in the eyes, he announce sharply:

'Father, I won't dig anymore!'

It's Domenico's turn to stop, he wipes his moustache with the cuff of his overall and at last decides to question his son:

'What's the matter with you? Is there something wrong?'

'No! I won't dig anymore. There are other jobs...'

All the evening he will not utter a word fearing anything he might say will make him change his mind.

However there seems nothing left to say. Fausto doesn't want to do peasant's work any longer.

The family get together; maybe he can he find a job in town? They enquire at friends and neighbours who sometimes go to the next town of Novi-Ligure. Eventually Uncle Giuseppe, after a visit there, discovers a Mr. Ettore, a pork butcher, is looking for a youngster to deliver his produce by bicycle. It now seems Fausto is going to become a butchers boy!

'One cool spring morning', he will recall, 'I took to the road taking my lunch in a big checked handkerchief and my brother Livio's bike . What a bicycle ! A huge machine, very heavy with tyres that belong to the rescue tugs in Genoa harbour'. His father accompanied him part of the way before he went about his work in the fields.

'Try and behave, my boy' he tells his son before he turns round to wipe the tears which run down his face.

Fausto has left. Castellania is becoming smaller behind him. He climbs the hill standing on the pedals, happy to ride with the sort of exhilaration produced by the sensation of freedom. In about twenty kilometres the profile of Novi-Ligure will appear, and eventually become a turning point in his destiny.

'Butcher's boy'

At 'Mr Ettore's', life is not always easy. Using an old bicycle, Coppi delivers the packets made up at the butcher's shop and he has to sleep in a small storeroom where during the winter it is freezing, as is the water he has to use to wash. He wakes up early, has a wash and goes about his work. On Sunday he goes home, riding through Cassano-Spinola, Villalvernia, and up the hills of Carezzano and Castel. At Castellania, he always meets his mother who is coming back from the mass in San Biagio.

Already he thinks about a job that would be more comfortable, and more lucrative too. In Novi-Ligure, Domenico Merlani is a pork butcher better known than 'Mr Ettore'. His trade is a lot bigger. Fausto learns that he is looking for a youngster to help out and applies for the job. He gets it.

His duties don't really change that much. Domenico Merlani makes up similar packets as 'Signor Ettore', wraps Parma ham, sausage, mortadella, ravioli and the young Coppi climbs hundreds of stairs every day. The shop assistant is satisfied with the modest tips his customers give him.

It has been arranged that the new delivery boy would board at Mr Merlani's with the promise that he can go home to Castellania every Sunday. However Fausto is bored at Novi-Ligure. He wants to go home every night. The urge to ride his bike is getting to him.

Eventually the boss agrees to his wishes. A pot-bellied man, sometime jovial, sometime uncouth, he does however threaten his shop assistant with a good hiding if he doesn't show up every morning at the shop at quarter to nine.

A new life starts.

'It's six! shouts his mother from the bottom of the stairs. Get up, Faustino, if you want to get to work on time.'

He will admit to being lazy and getting up late despite the awful noise that the old alarm clock makes. On the road to Novi-Ligure he will race against the clock, often trying to stay in the slipstream of a truck in order to arrive in time. Despite still being sleepy when leaving the village, his strong and determined style soon permits him to gets into a good rhythm.

The idea of cycle racing starts to appeal to him and Merlani's shop is often used as a meeting place for the other local cyclists. There, they often talk about Costante Girardengo's achievements, the first of the really great Italian champions and a local as well. A complete racing cyclist, 'Milan-San Remo' was 'his' race, winning it six times, as indeed was the national championship which he won no less than nine years in succession! He was also twice winner of the Tour of Italy and three times victor in the Tour of Lombardy. To the young Coppi, Girardengo was some kind of 'God' and he doesn't even dare to dream that one day he will actually meet him.

The baker's boy from the bakery next door boasts about meeting 'the big Constante' while delivering panetone for his boss. Fausto really wants to meet great champion but doesn't think he will ever be that lucky.

But one day his boss calls to him.

'Ride to Girardengo's house and take him a salami!'

Usually it's Merlani himself who takes care of that glorious job. This day, however he is too busy but the young teenager of Castellania thinks for an instant it's all a joke. His heart starts to beat hard and he probably will never again climb on his bike so fast as he did that day.

The meeting doesn't go well, the great champion cyclist looks at young Coppi with a harsh eye then reproaches him for the way he handles the goods. Disappointed, young Coppi clears from his mind the myth of Girardengo.

However, he continues to show boundless energy which will not escape his employers attention. He will often say for all to hear:

'The kid is less sickly than he appears. He accomplishes his job well, rides from morning to evening and evidently when it's time to go to bed, he is as fresh as when he wakes up'

Fausto has just turned fifteen. His muscles are growing and getting stronger. Every day, when riding back and forth to work, he always tries to beat his own record for the trip.

One day while riding alone he suddenly finds himself amongst a group of cyclists out training. He is eager to join in and decides to try and keep up with them. This fills him with excitement and wonder. The cyclists ride at quite a pace on light bikes with tubular tyres. Fausto looks at the equipment in awe. What beautiful machines!

He will always remember this particular occasion and the cyclist who was joking with his friend Mario about the skinny kid riding his grandfather's bike but still somehow able to follow the group.

Upset at the remarks, Coppi made a deliberate and successful attempt to stay with the group for a while. For the first time, the 'poor little boy', became aware of his abilities.

But they are right to talk about his old bicycle. Fausto dreams of a beautiful bicycle that he admires every day in a shop window in Novi. Chrome shining, it's a 'Legnano' one of the best known brands in the country.

'I really think, admited Fausto, many years later, that if one had ask me to cut out a few years of my life to get it, I would have give them up without batting an eyelid. 'Legnano' was the brand of Gino Bartali, my God, whose picture cut from a newspaper had pride of place in my bedroom. I never dared to go in the shop and even touch the frame with my hands. I contented myself with looking at it and with wondering by which miracle I could become the owner of it.'

Eventually a member of the family comes to his rescue. It is not his Uncle Giuseppe but another whose name is also Fausto Coppi. An officer in the Merchant Navy, when he makes the trip from Genoa to Castellania wearing his splendid uniform the visit is held in high esteem by his relatives in the village.

At the beginning of 1935, he arrives at the village and is greeted by his family including all his nephews and nieces. He relentlessly questions young Fausto about his job but his nephew can only speak about cycle racing and how he can match the local 'racers' on their training rides despite not having a proper racing bike like the others. The boy is aware that a racing machine is expensive but thinks if he can buy a frame, he could borrow a pair of wheels.

He talks unceasingly to his Uncle about his future plans and his 'performances'. His uncle is deeply moved and impressed by the youngster's enthusiasm.

When he goes back to the sea, he leaves a little bit of money with his brother Domenico to help with the household expenses. A much appreciated gesture in those difficult times. But during his long hours of loneliness, Uncle Fausto is going to think and think again about his young nephew's passion. Why shouldn't he help him to buy the bicycle of his dreams?

When the ship stops at Ceylon he has made up his mind, he writes firmly to his brother:

'I am sending you four hundred liras. Add the difference and finally buy Faustino the bicycle he deserves. Who knows one day he might become a real racing cyclist?'

Uncle Fausto who bought the future champion his first bicycle

Fausto Coppi at the time of one of his first victories in the amateur ranks (1939)

A young Coppi (centre) A butcher's boy... not yet a top cyclist!

A miracle has just happened ! Fausto's father, because of such a grand gesture from his brother somehow finds the extra one hundred and seventy liras needed to buy the bicycle. Fausto has already asked at Bovone's shop the price of the machine he wanted. The bicycle costs exactly five hundred and seventy liras.

With the money in his hands, he rushes to town and comes back even faster to Castellania with his new purchase, a real racing bike with the frame painted in a light enamel.

Fausto can't wait to take part in the local races for non-licensed riders. One of them is to welcome back soldiers from oriental Africa, the organisers have arranged an event which winds through the hills on a circuit that takes in Castellania, Costa Vescovato, Villa Romagnano and Tortona. Fausto Coppi triumphs and wins twenty liras and a salami sausage. His uncle Guiseppe greets him at the finish and whispers to him:

'If you try hard enough, the only work you have to do will be on the bike'

And the young winner is going to try hard. With his success comes the desire to get an even lighter frame. Alas, things don't go exactly according to plan...

Some friends give him the address of a frame-builder whose business is in Asti. He decides to take the train to the town and rushes to the shop.

The young Fausto hasn't yet developed much business sense. So to get his frame as soon as possible, he thinks it's best to pay right away. As a consequence of his rash actions his frame will never be finished. He makes the trip to Asti no less than seven times to be told every time that he'll have to come back.

Every time he returns he finds it hard to hold back the tears, not daring to tell people who see him that he is crying just because of a bicycle frame.

Eventually, to get rid of the persistent young customer, the builder gives him a frame from stock which doesn't even fit.

Despite this setback Fausto will still win many other races.

The lucky hunchback

IF FAUSTO COPPI'S FACE REFLECTS AN IMPRESSION OF THINNESS, his physical structure is, on the other hand, sturdy and his lean muscles are developing impressively. He often trains up to a hundred kilometres while still working at Merlani's. If he has a spare hour he will spend it improving his condition.

Work and cycling, that is his life. Nothing else counts, but in his heart it is riding his bike that is more important than his work.

He has already won a race and this victory has made a big impression in his village. Castellania's people are now interested in him, following his progress and discussing his possibilities of success. His father Domenico feels very proud when he hears his son could have all the qualities for a big career in cycling racing. Despite this he feels people might be a little quick in their judgement.

At the beginning of 1938, Fausto takes out an official amateur licence. The serious stage is about to start. His father accepts that he will have to leave his job to stay at Castellania full time, but his mother is reluctant. Being home will not mean Fausto just rides his bike and devotes himself to training, his father makes it clear right away: Fausto will help with the work in the fields but will be free to train when he has to. Even so his mother is not happy and as races go by becomes irritable. She still can't stand the idea that her son left his job to become a racing cyclist.

'You never win!' She tells him.

Yet Fausto does win his first race, as a licence holder this time, at Castelletto d'Orba, in the Novi-Ligure district. He rode with all the experience of an older rider: staying with the bunch until the route became difficult, then attacked leaving everybody behind and won alone. This victory was a great boost for his morale. You can feel the birth of a champion is near.

His father and Livio were there at the race, overjoyed with Fausto's success. They made him recount to them numerous times how he rode to victory. In his lunch bag, he has the prize: a nice looking alarm-clock which he gives to his mother. She handles it with joy turning it around and around in her hands almost with disbelief, then puts it proudly on the chimney mantelpiece.

The clock set on a small statue in the shape of a hunchback attracts a remark from aunt Albina:

'That's a good start, Fausto! This small hunchback will bring you luck.'

The race prizes are mostly given as goods and Fausto is not really earning any money. He often has to leave Castellania with just a few goat cheese sandwiches and ride eighty kilometres to the start of a race two hundred kilometres long.

'Once a race finished,' he'll remember, 'I had ride home by bicycle, because I never had enough money to rent a room overnight, not even a cheap one. Cars were rare at the time but anyway no one would have given a lift to an emaciated teenager named Fausto Coppi'.

He will later confide to Gaston Benac, the first French journalist who will meet him the day after the armistice:

'Sometimes, to enable me to take part in a race, I needed ten or twenty liras to pay for the journey and we just didn't have those ten or twenty liras. One day, my brother Livio, who had a blind faith in me, withdrew all his savings from the bank and gave them to me. Sometimes I only had a little money for the journey and to buy food so I would take half a dozen hard boiled eggs. At the beginning of 1939, I had to spend twenty liras to go to a race in Turin but I crashed a few kilometres before the finish. Another trip cost me thirty liras and I fell again, broke a wheel and had to retire from the race. What was I to do, give up?'

He will keep trying and will confide later:

'I don't regret anything of that part of my life. It was necessary to the birth, within myself, of this burning need to succeed socially, to reach something better than what was waiting for me in Castellania... I understand perfectly that a boy raised in a upper class environment cannot submit himself to the strict discipline which alone can create a tough rider able to turn a blind eye to his disadvantages.'

But lets go back to the whirlwind of races.

When Fausto was working at Merlani's, his boss was often visited in the back of the shop, by an enigmatic and colourful man called Giuseppe - nicknamed Biagio - Cavanna. A famous masseur and former top boxer, he had also been the trainer of Costante Girardengo and was in great demand by all the top teams. He was known as 'The one that can work miracles' , 'the wizard of the muscles'.

When Cavanna visited Merlani's he used to sit down on a crate and talk at length. In front of an attentive audience, he would recall in detail the achievements of racing cyclists he knew, always straight and to the point he would talk of an athlete's physical constitution and where precisely such and such rider was getting his strength from.

Fausto would soak up the big man's words and take in anything he said. He would be a champion one day, it was his one ambition and nothing could sway him from his chosen path. He really wanted to talk to the masseur, to confide in him his plans for the future but never dared to, fearing the famous trainer would just laugh at him.

Cavanna had his own brood in Pozzolo Formigaro near Lovi-Ligure. He was keeping under his wing, riders that he had selected himself. Isodoro Bergaglio was in Cavanna's team and used to go to Merlani's to do the trainer's shopping. There, he often met Coppi. They became friends and started training together with Fausto, learning as much as possible from the technique of his new companion.

On their rides together Coppi used to give Bergaglio a hard time. Isodoro was so impressed he told Cavanna about his talented new friend. The trainer didn't pay much attention he just knew that Bergaglio was talking about the 'tall skinny boy from Merlani's'.

In 1938, Cavanna had something tragic happen to him. He suddenly became blind. From then on he wore black glasses and used the white stick of the blind. However, his abilities won't be diminished.

'My hands', he would readily confide, with a tender pride, 'see better than any human eye and my ears hear sounds that are unknown to you. My hands and my ears never lie. The pulse reveals to me the quality of the heart and the voice tells me the virtues or the vices of the character. It's with the muscles of the neck and back that I come to appreciate the strengths of a rider'.

In 1938, Coppi meets Cavanna for the first time, introduced by another of his pupils: Domenico Semenza.

In the trainer's den, his heart is racing fast. Cavanna! A god to a racing cyclist. Fausto is apprehensive because of all the things he has been told about the blind man's temperament: his gruff manner and sudden and violent rages. Yet when Cavanna courteously greets him, his fears disappear and Coppi learns that this big man really has the heart of a child. Biagio Cavanna immediately shows great kindness for the young rider.

'He knew how to tell me which path to take', Fausto recalled later. 'The one of consciousness, seriousness and honesty. Never short of suggestions, he will start to guide me physically and psychologically, when my self confidence threaten to crumble. That way, intelligently, he will encourage me to follow the difficult way I had decided for myself.'

The 1938 season is nearing its end. The young man from Piedmont hasn't pulled off any big result yet but, despite this disappointment, he retains all the confidence of his trainer.

1939 - His twentieth year opens on an optimistic note when on a

February day, Cavanna suggests he leaves the amateur ranks and take out an Independent licence. This will enable him on occasion to race with the professionals.

Fausto realises suddenly that his trainer had just shown great trust in his abilities.

Alas, success is not forthcoming.

'You have to wait and persist', Cavanna always says. 'Be brave. This is the moment of the biggest sacrifices. You'll see ; one day you'll reap the reward of your work. Don't let yourself be affected by the critics, you will succeed, I am sure of it!'

Moreover, Cavanna wasn't being lenient. In April he sends Coppi to Florence, to ride the Tour of Toscane but gives him very little tactical advice.

'No plan, you follow Bartali, that's all'

But of course to follow Bartali is no easy task. The race route includes many hard climbs on which Coppi holds his own and would have kept up with Bartali had he not been stopped by a broken wheel after hundred and forty kilometres on the climb at Prunetta.

He begs, in vain, for the race directors of the event to give him another wheel, but with tears in his eyes, he has to climb into the broom wagon and go humbly back to Florence.

The 7th of May 1939, he finally triumphs winning at Varzi, in one of the series of races that make up the Independent Championship of Italy.

On the difficult climb at Penice, he rides away alone and leaves all the favourites far behind. He eventually finishes nearly seven minutes ahead of the next rider. He follows this with another win at Pavie, this time with a lead of six minutes. These are seen as remarkable victories.

Already it is predicted that Coppi's season will be outstanding. Cavanna is so convinced about his potential that he wants him to ride the Tour of Piedmont classic. He will be the local lad up against all the big professional stars. What a test !!

ON FAMILIAR TERMS WITH THE IDOLS

IN THE AREA AROUND NOVI LIGURE, Costante Girardengo ran a cycling team called the 'Maino' which had scored some convincing successes. But relations between the ex-champion and Biagio Cavanna were rather cool. The blind masseur didn't appreciate the authoritarian methods of the 'Great Costante' who, on his own admission, 'knew everything, and had seen it all.' In passing, the masseur had put Coppi on his guard:

'Don't let that man come near you,' he had said.

This remark only served to confirm what young Fausto already felt in his own mind, because, as we have seen, the former idol's manner had not gone down well with him on a visit he paid as a butcher's boy.

There things rested until, returning from a long training ride a few days before the Tour of Piedmont,, who should Coppi find installed in his living room but the same Costante Girardengo in person, chatting away to his mother and father. He had, of course, only just dropped by – but to some purpose: the barefaced proposition of a contract tying Coppi to his own set-up. Fausto felt both flattered and ill-at-ease to discover this former 'Campionissimo' putting himself out on his behalf. The incident of Merlani's salami was put behind them. Who knows if Girardengo even remembers it? As for Coppi's parents, it's as if God has descended from the heavens to their humble abode. What's more, he is obviously taken with their son. The 'Great Costante' is there among them.

Domenico and Angiolina can hardly believe their eyes, for not only is he truly present but he has brought a contract. All Fausto has to do is sign, there at the bottom of the page.

'Go on, Fausto, sign – it's for Mr Girardengo.'

And of course he pens his name, albeit hesitantly. How could he say no?

The crafty old directeur sportif, content with the stroke he has just pulled, doesn't hang around. He waves goodbye to the family, pats Fausto on the back and quits Castellania, stirring up a cloud of dust behind his little red sports car.

Calm reigns again in the village. But not for Coppi. Behind the green shutters he knows that he hasn't acted in good faith towards Cavanna, who has him bound by a moral contract at least. The news reaches his mentor a few hours later.

Night falls. There is a gleam of headlights, a screech of brakes; an ominous black shadow alights from a car. It is Cavanna.

"Where is Girardengo," he bellows, "so's I can break my stick across his back. What a little swine you are, Fausto. After all I've done for you. I got you in with Santamaria, the bike builders, so that they could help you along and now you betray me."

Cavanna couldn't give two hoots for the 'Maino' contract. Had he not already written to Eberardo Pavesi, the directeur sportif at 'Legnano,' Bartali's sponsors, alerting them to young Coppi's great class?

Now he would have to start all over again. Cavanna makes such a fuss that Fausto's father has to go and plead with Girardengo for the annulment of the try-out contract with 'Maino'.

Castellania's young rising star has seen out the storm. His elder brother Livio, and the younger Serse, are completely bewildered; they'd seen the big blind man bang his fist on the table. Then once he'd swept away, like a hurricane amidst the cackling of frightened hens, peace returns to the little village in all its eventide fullness.

Fausto has other worries. He is suffering from an awkwardly placed boil, a complaint with which racing cyclists are only too familiar, but manages to hide his anxiety.

On the 4th June 1939, at the start of the Tour of Piedmont, sporting the canary yellow jersey of Santamaria of Novi, number ninety-eight sneaks a glance at Bartali, the impassive Gino, an internationally acclaimed star, winner of the previous year's Tour of France. Gino stands out; with his haughty bearing he is already head and shoulders above the sheeplike peloton whose only wish is to follow in his tracks.

From the off Fausto is fearful, apprehensive about the prospect of rubbing shoulders with the elite, an enterprise he doesn't really feel up to. He always felt this sense of being out of place in his first contacts with the real aces, something which only left him as the kilometres rolled by. So when the race began to approach its final stages and despite the suffocating heat, he had regained his strength, all his bounding energy.

With sixty kilometres to go, he found himself part of a very distinguished leading group which included: Bartali, Vicini, Valetti and the Italian champion, Bizzi. A state of affairs which did wonders for his confidence. He decided, therefore, to play his strongest card and attack as they went through Castelnuovo – a daring move. A little climb presented itself, Fausto was out of the saddle and away. Seeing nothing in front or hearing nothing from behind, he pursued his effort over several kilometres. When eventually he looks back he's made the break. There is only forty kilometres to go to the finish. He is alone in the lead, him, the little 'independent' with the look of a scrawny bird of prey, the former butcher's boy dominating the cream of the international pro peloton in the arduous Tour of Piedmont.

The nearer he came to the Turin velodrome the more he was absorbed by the dream of finishing on his own. Fausto could already hear the shouts of the crowd, who were actually expecting Bartali, but would greet instead the arrival of a thin youth, utterly unknown, decked out in a jersey drained of all colour by the ravages of sweat and dust.

The dream, alas, dissolved in an instant. Towards the top of the long climb of Moriondo – one of the major difficulties – Fausto's chain unships. There is no alternative but to stop. He gets off his bike and over-hastily replaces the chain on a cog which leaves him in too high a gear, in no way appropriate to the steepness of the gradient. Back on his bike again he is balanced stock-still leaning over the pedals when Bartali bursts through from behind. 'Gino the Great, Gino the Mystic,' has caught him napping.

Bartali shoots a surprised glance in the newcomer's direction. Where did this one come from? Never seen him before. The Tuscan takes the opportunity to attack. The unknown counters, latching onto his back wheel. At this point Bartali's astonishment is complete. He looks Coppi over again, unable to believe his eyes and then asks him to work in the break, a group which also includes the dark haired Del Cancia, the sprinter Leoni and the current national champion, Olimpio Bizzi – all of whom are tucked in behind Bartali. Coppi doesn't have to be asked twice.

There he is then, crossing swords with Bartali for the first time.

While the battle moves on to rage on the slopes of the Rezza pass, the honours of this first duel go to the Florentine old master.

Coppi holds Del Cancia until half-way up the climb and then gives him best. He finishes third.

In the Turin velodrome, Bartali comes face to face with the stranger in the yellow jersey.

'Bravo, you rode well,' he mutters.

That is all. Fausto, gratified nonetheless, is scanning the crowd for a single face — that of Biagio Cavanna.

'I found him,' he recounted later, "sitting on his own, motionless, his unlit eyes full of tears.'

'You see, Fausto, I was right.'

They hugged each other long and hard under the gaze of Santamaria and Fiorelli, his other mentors, who had taken it upon themselves to provide all his equipment for that day.

Afterwards Coppi and Cavanna went to the hotel where the Legnano team, including Bartali, were based. A contract was quickly signed stipulating that Coppi would ride during 1940 for the sum of seven hundred lira a month – with an option to renew – as a team-mate (i.e. domestique) to Bartali.

From then on he was bouyed up with much greater confidence.

As an independent, he picked up wins at Arezzo, in Genoa, and then on the 14th August at Varese. This last race was particularly close to his heart. Run off on the Three Valleys of Varese circuit, over a hundred and eighty kilometres, it invariably produced a winner who was a good all-rounder.

There was a slight hitch on the starting line.

Coppi presented in the rather washed out colours of the team he was riding for at that time, the 'Tortona Working Men's Club' who were hardly rich. If there had been a best dressed prize he would have been eliminated straight away.

In the event that almost happened. General Antonellli, who was president of the Italian Cycling Federation, pointed out to him that such a turnout was unworthy of a race which counted towards the national independent championship. However, he took into consideration the fact that the rider was not wholly responsible for his garb and let him start anyway.

Coppi lined up boiling inside with rage. This Varese Grand Prix was so demanding that the winner was considered to be the moral victor of the Italian championship. (NB: The title of Independent Champion of Italy was decided on points over several races. However, Coppi knew that he could not win because he had not taken part in all the counting events. Cavanna was of the opinion that such a title would bring him no great return, preferring to hold him in reserve for other more telling races where he could line up with the professionals.)

Coppi rode his usual race. Everything fell into place for him. When the time came to attack he was out of the saddle and dropped all the other members of the break he had slipped away with. After that it was simply a matter of cruising home on his own. He had shown himself to be in a class above the rest of the field.

Alfonso Spinelli, a columnist in the Gazzetta dello Sport talked of, 'the clearcut superiority of the Castellania rider. There could be little doubt that the best man won. Nobody could touch Coppi.'

From the outset the same pattern was apparent in the way Coppi won his races. His intelligence, his timing, rarely let him down. He knew where and when to put in his effort. He was already riding like a champion.

That victory in Varese was a turning point in his career. He would remember it for the rest of his life for one simple reason: it was 1939 and war cries were beginning to be heard all over Europe.

In the little inn where he celebrated his win there was a certain unrest. Vendors in the street outside were announcing hot news. Someone picked up the latest edition of the 'Stampa Sera' fresh in from Turin. War had been declared.

Italy was not yet involved, and for the moment Coppi could continue to increase his tally of wins. He mixed with the professionals again and beat Bartali in a track pursuit which formed part of the 'Stampa-Fiat' grand prix. In a similar race he went down to Olimpio Bizzi.

The 'Gazzetta dello Sport' of the 14th November 1939, under the byline of Guido Giardini, devoted a special section to him – the first of many such – beneath the headline, "Up and coming men in cycling," which said in substance:

'Fausto Coppi, who came to the sporting life rather timidly and without any great pretensions, seemed to be another addition to the great troop of young hopefuls. Nobody thought he had the physical ability or any potential to rank with the big names…

Coppi is just twenty years old. He was born on the land which has given the sport many great champions. In only five months he has already made such progress along the way that the public and half of Italy has been won over. How far will he go?'

THE MASTERSTROKE

FOR THE YOUNG NEO-PRO A NEW CHAPTER OPENED. War raged across a great part of Europe, but as yet Italy had been spared the dreadful scourge.

He is meticulous about putting Biagio Cavanna's instructions into practice.

In the morning the alarm goes off at five o'clock. An hour later he has breakfast and leaves Castellania for Novi Ligure or Tortona.

After this stretching of the legs, he returns home at nine – with the exception of intensive training days, on Wednesday and Friday, when he puts in sorties of a hundred and eighty to two hundred kilometres.

Once back he takes a bath, with a few litres of vinegar added, in a tub –a separate bathroom is still the stuff of dreams – which is placed in the dining room.

At midday he sits down to eat. On the menu: mixed starters, especially tuna, sardines or raw ham, then soup, meat and salad. He often has some grapes because the family has a small trellised vine. Wine is forbidden. From time to time though, just to please his mother, he will accept half a glass. More often he takes a quarter bottle of beer.

After a siesta between two and four he has a light collation of tea and rusks before another training ride.

At about seven thirty dinner consists of soup, half a chicken with salad or cooked vegetables and stewed fruit.

By ten Fausto is in bed, the shutters closed, but the window open.

Cavanna makes it clear to his pupil that in order to become a true roadman, one worthy of opening a bank account, he would have to give up all pleasures, especially those of the table.

Coppi always remembered the kilos of salad he used to devour during those days.

His coach also added the rejoinder that he should never tire of riding his bike. That's how you become a 'Great,' he would say. On the other hand, he insisted that a racing cyclist should never go for walks. And Fausto was to find out for himself that after long hunting trips and the resultant stiffness in his legs that he would be obliged to spend prolonged sessions on his pedalling machine – the home trainer.

Lastly, Cavanna recommended the ideal sleeping position: stretched out on the right side with the left leg drawn up to the centre of the body, as if riding the bike.

"It was a tough regime," Fausto acknowledged. "But every time I thought of giving up I remembered the life of toil on the farm."

The young professional passed through many periods of despondency in the early months of 1940. Wins and places were rather scarce.

Pavesi, after the manner of Cavanna, reassured his new protégé:

'Don't you worry about results,' he muttered, his pipe clenched firmly between yellowing teeth, 'as long as you've got class they will come in their own good time.'

Behind the scenes, preparations were going ahead for the event that the sporting public were eagerly awaiting, the Tour of Italy – the famous Giro. Coppi would take part in the Legnano team by the side of his leader, Bartali, and his team-mates Magni, Favalli, Ricci, Secondo, Ronconi and Succi.

Although he had gained admittance to the top echelon and nothing much was expected of him, his morale was by no means high. The period of doubt continued. At home in Castellania, in the bosom of the family, he found a little peace and decided that whatever happened he would not let the occasion slip by. That he would give it all he had in him however much the distance, was cause for concern – but he would do it to spite all the wagging tongues who were suggesting, behind his back, that he might do better to return to Merlani's cooked meats. He decided to make all possible efforts to secure victory for his leader, Bartali. Gino would have the whole team behind him with the exception of Magni and Favalli who were to try for stage victories.

This was June 1940. Italy had still not committed herself to war. The cannons roared for a few hours on the Franco-Italian border, but for the mainland as a whole it was only a phoney war. Throughout the peninsula most people's attention was drawn towards the twenty eighth Tour of Italy which started in Milan on the 19th May. Fausto should have been in uniform at the time, but the authorities had consented to a thirty day deferment so that he could take part in the race.

Most of the predictions were for Bartali, but there was another favourite; Valetti – winner of the race for the past two years – who rode for the rival Bianchi team. Everything was therefore set for a momentous struggle between Legnano and Bianchi. The majority, however, were behind Bartali. He was the darling of the crowd, they had eyes for him alone, he was the only one they wanted to cheer.

Unfortunately a crash on the descent of the Scoffera during the second stage from Turin to Genoa robbed him of practically any chance of final victory. Coppi, on the other hand, came in second on the stage.

Two days later, from Pisa to Grossetto, Bartali was still feeling the effects of his crash. Coppi, however, was flying. Up ahead he saw a break developing and felt ready to go with them. But he hesitated, thinking of his team captain. Unable to hold back any longer, he drew alongside Pavesi's car to ask permission to take off. The directeur sportif was put on the spot. Should he continue to protect Bartali, the standard bearer of the whole nation, while he had everything to gain by letting Coppi have his head? What was he to do? On one side he made a grimace for Bartali as if to say: 'Coppi is to stay where he is,' at the same time on the other giving Fausto the all clear with a gesture: On your way, attack.

And Fausto took off, caught the leaders, but was struck down by bad luck; one of his cranks broke, then his saddle frame snapped three hundred metres from the finishing line. A few precious seconds were lost which fortunately did nothing to prevent him hoisting himself to second place overall behind his team-mate Favalli.

From then on he was confidence itself whatever misfortune seemed to stick to his wheels. He crashed, equipment broke under him, but he had the wholehearted backing of his directeur sportif.

"Ride your own race," he told him. "Break away as soon as you sense danger. You're nobody's team-mate, understand? You've got the wind behind you. The others will let you get on with it, they won't take any notice.

Pavesi laid it on the line for the whole team:

'Coppi won't be a water carrier any more. From now on, he's Bartali's right hand man.'

The latter had now lost all hope of victory while Coppi had yet to show what he was capable of. Every day he would sum up his opponent's strengths and no longer suffered from any sense of inferiority towards them, even that little chap Mollo who was currently wearing the pink jersey of leadership.

The eleventh stage included some big climbs, notably the Albertone pass. It was there that Coppi would have to go on the offensive if he wanted to win the Giro.

He was excellently placed on general classification, only three minutes behind the leader, and he had Pavesi's complete confidence.

The weather was terrible from the start which added to the difficulty of the stage but did not stop attacks coming thick and fast. Fausto, ever watchful, bided his time. Bartali had been left behind; he could not keep up with the pace.

One man climbed the Abertone pass alone in the lead, Ezio Cecchi. In his wake, a little group chased, notable for the presence of Fausto Coppi. Pavesi soon drew level with him. The moment had come for his rider to show what he was made of.

He went on the attack; once, twice, three times he launched a brutal offensive and eventually got away to pursue the lone rider in the lead. Despite the heavy rain, which turned into sleet as the summit approached, Fausto was feeling peculiarly strong in himself and was brimming with confidence. Before long Cecchi was caught and immediately dropped. Back down the road, the chase was coming together. Fausto held on. Better still, he began to increase his lead over the final climbs, the Barigazzo and the Montefestino, to arrive at Modena in triumph with nearly four minutes in hand over the first of the chasers. From that moment he was the overall leader and thus put on the coveted pink jersey. It was no longer a dream.

The Giro, however, is long. A dozen stages remained, with the Dolomites still to cross. Every day required a constant vigilance. The new pink jersey was not at all flustered and revealed a hitherto unsuspected side to his character, countering all attempts at escape, and nipping in the bud the least hint of a coalition.

Bartali lost more and more ground. At the end of the fifteenth stage, where the Dolomites began, Coppi and a group of fugitives left him behind to the tune of half an hour. A situation which was hardly to his liking, one could be sure, since he began to talk of abandoning. But Pavesi succeeded in persuading him that such a retreat would do nothing for his popularity while if he were to place himself at the disposal of his young water-carrier, Coppi, the public would applaud this gesture of self sacrifice.

Thus Bartali came to Coppi's aid in one of the subsequent Dolomite stages, when the latter was suffering from stomach ache, passing him a bottle, urging him on and generally helping him through the crisis. Fausto showed a lively appreciation and Bartali continued in this role of adviser during the next few stages.

The Giro was all but over. The last stage, Verona to Milan, was a triumphal procession. For Fausto, however, it just missed being a drama. An slipped chain brought him to a halt within sight of the finish. He entered the densely packed Milan Arena thirty seconds behind the main bunch, his face covered in grime. But it was no time for waving to the crowd. The Giro was his, as he finished ahead of Mollo at 2 minutes 40 seconds, with Cottur third at 11 minutes 45 seconds. Bartali took ninth place at 45 minutes.

All the family, with the exception of mamma, made the journey from Castellania to embrace Fausto who had become a national hero.

In the Gazzetta dello Sport of the 10th June, Bruno Roghi wrote:'The Tour of Italy has not been won by a rider broken in by the school of hard knocks, by all the demands and pitfalls of a tough career, but by a lowly conscript on leave, and the Italian sporting public has got wind of a new and forceful talent.'

On the evening of the great day, Fausto returned to the village to embrace his mother who was crying with joy.

"Are you tired?" She asked, trembling with emotion. Then she burst into tears, and her son with her.

In the Tour of Italy (1940), Coppi (right) has become the leader, upsetting the plans of Bartali (centre) who scarcely seems to be appreciating the situation

Preparations for a duel.

Two days after his brilliant victory, Italy's new star changed his pink jersey for a duller garb. As he had been sent to the Giro on the orders of the military authorities, all he had to do when he got back to barracks was click his heels, salute, and offer the traditional report: "Mission accomplished, Sir."

Drafted into the 38th Tortona Infantry with the number 7375, he was soon transferred to Limone-Piemonte, then back to Tortona. There he underwent the basic training common to all conscripts, drawing his rifle and applying himself to arms drill.

'I could not get used to that killing machine,' he afterwards lamented, 'much less to the idea that one day I might have to use it against others, perhaps boys of my own age. The idea haunted and revolted me.

If I couldn't abide my rifle, the same went for my grey-green uniform and all the rest of the barbaric clutter, both uncomfortable and noisy, which was the standard issue to a soldier of his majesty Victor Emmanuel: the helmet, the water bottle, the mess tin, the belts, and the number one, two and three uniforms. During the inspections I would always be short of something, and four to five times a day I'd have trouble with my puttees.'

Coppi could hardly complain, though, about his first few months of army life. His superiors had promised to let him train and compete in races. The only condition being that he should be back in barracks for the evening roll-call.

The Italian pursuit championships had a place in his programme because he wanted to learn track-craft and prove himself capable of playing a major role on the indoor tracks as well as on the road.

The 30th June 1940 found him appearing at Milan's Vigorelli track. Without the least hitch he was able to reach the final of a speciality which was not altogether his. He only began to appreciate the difficulty when he made ready to confront the title holder, Olimpio Bizzi. Faced with the king of this particular discipline, one might have expected some feeling of inferiority but, on the contrary, Coppi seemed quietly confident. To be sure he had already been beaten by Bizzi in Turin, but only just. Moreover, after his victory in the Tour of Italy, he had picked up a crowd of fans who had come to the Vigorelli to show their support.

A hush fell upon the audience before the start, the whole place held its breath. The starter's pistol sounded. Bizzi shot away like an arrow and gained several metres advantage. Fausto was not flustered however. Taking his time, he fought back and forced the man from Livorno into a huge effort to maintain his lead, an effort which was to prove fatal. From then on Coppi knew that not only was he holding his own but that he could, if he wanted, accelerate and gain ground in his turn. This was the tactic he put into operation. The crowd sensed his intention and was already on its feet cheering him on. They knew that the man they were acclaiming was a complete all-rounder, capable of winning on the track as well as on the road. In the end he took the victory with thirty metres in hand over his opponent and in so doing became Italian pursuit champion. It was his first official title. His rise to stardom had been dazzling.

This success ushered in one of those periods in his life which he considered to be completely happy. He had left behind a youth in which poverty was his daily lot, when hunger sometimes gnawed at him as he enviously watched those who could satisfy their every need.

On the military front, his superiors continued to show the tolerance that we have previously noted. He lined up in the Tour of Lombardy side by side with Bartali who was still the nation's idol. That year already, 1940, he had won Milan San Remo, the Tours of Tuscany and Campania plus the Grand Prix of Rome. The Tour of Lombardy was the last event counting towards the Italian championship which was judged on points but Bartali had amassed such a lead that he was unbeatable in the final classification. Coppi, however, would not accept the superiority of the man who was gradually becoming his direct rival. And during the event he gave ample proof of his claims to parity, but misfortune prevented him from winning, which left the way open once again for a triumphant Bartali.

Coppi found many offers coming in from abroad. His superiors would let him go, but for a short time only. He accepted an invitation from some promoters in Zurich to come and see how he measured up against the rising star of the Swiss scene, Ferdi Kubler, who was the same age as himself.

Fausto quickly packed a suitcase, the bike being sent on ahead courtesy of Legnano, and took the first train for Switzerland.

'Arriving in front of the Oerliken velodrome,' he recounted, 'I proudly presented myself at the door of the rider's quarters.

'What can I do for you, young man?' The porter inquired rather haughtily.

I mumbled a few vague words in Italian of which he fastened upon the only two that he recognised: Fausto Coppi.

As he was well acquainted with the evening's programme, his face lit up and he let me in.'

On that 8th December, the velodrome was full to bursting point. The Zurich fans had come to watch their hero see off in record time this interloper whom the Italians were already touting as a new champion but who was, to all intents, an unknown quantity abroad and furthermore an 'unknown' who didn't really feel too sure of himself beyond his own frontiers. He was ill at ease before this crowd which had gathered with the sole aim of witnessing his defeat. The ball was in his court; it was up to him to topple the idol of the Swiss sporting public.

The starter fired his pistol. The infernal chase was on. At the same time a roar went up, issuing from the top of thousands of lungs: Kubler, Kubler. Both men were bent over their machines, their noses brushing the handlebars, while they pushed themselves to the limit, gaining and losing a few metres one after another. It was a fierce struggle.

All of a sudden though, the man who should have been reeled in seemed to throw the hook and the reeler faltered. From that moment a tragedy was set in motion. Kubler lost more and more ground. He had shot his bolt. Coppi upped the pace a little more and the Swiss found himself being steadily brought back. In no time Kubler was dangling only a few metres in front of the Italian - on the verge of the worst dishonour being overtaken before the full regulation five thousand metres had been covered. Then it was over, he was caught.

Coppi would always remember that moment:

'A kind of drama began to unfold before my eyes. The entire audience rose as one, dumb struck, as if turned to stone; and a fearful hush, complete and utter silence, chilling even, fell upon the velodrome.'

Fausto had conquered in Zurich-Oerliken.

As usual he returned to barracks. He seemed happy passing through the guard house and his room-mates looked at him with envious eyes. All they had before them was the tedious prospect of going on exercises, while Fausto had a free rein to follow the great joy of his life, cycle racing.

Another great joy had come into his life, happiness pure and simple. Love popped up without warning. While out training he had several times come across a young girl by the side of the road but had never yet managed to say a word to her. It was the same girl who, with a few of her friends, had come to ask for his autograph during a criterium after his victorious Tour of Italy. Things would have rested there but for a day in August 1940 – the 29th to be precise – when getting in the miles as usual, he came upon the young girl, whose name was Bruna

Ciampolini, once again on the road between Novi Ligure and Castellania. He was by nature timid, a timidity which was almost pathological. On that day, however, he could never understand what strange impulse compelled him to stop and engage in conversation.

As they walked side by side, Coppi learned that she lived in Sestri-Ponente, a seaside suburb of Genoa and that some of her family were living in Villalvernia, the cross-roads which led to the Castellania road.

The little Genoese questioned Fausto about his life as a racing cyclist. Up to then sport had hardly interested her. She nonetheless brought up the subject of the Tour of Italy and timorously admitted that she had only seen it once at La Spezia while she was still a child. She could even remember her terror at having seen Learco Guerra crash in front of her and get up covered in blood.

Love, in the shape of a brunette from the suburbs of Genoa, had entered the life of Fausto Coppi.

Fausto Coppi about to embark on his second year as a professional, in 1941

THE MOST PRESTIGIOUS RECORD

IN 1941, ITALY BEGAN TO FEEL THE EFFECTS OF A WAR IN WHICH SHE WAS NOT YET FULLY ENGAGED. As a result, the Tour of Italy disappeared from the fixture list. One-day races, on the other hand, continued to take place. So it came about that Coppi was able to show the full extent of his class in the Tour of Tuscany. He dropped Bartali, beating him on his own home ground in Florence to take his first 'classic' victory.

That Spring the rivalry between Coppi and Bartali began to really draw attention as Fausto more and more felt himself propelled towards the conquest of greater glory.

In the Tour of Veneto, having broken away with the excellent Cinelli, he attacked with three kilometres to go and finished on his own thus adding a touch of notoriety to his growing popularity. Bartali crossed the line more than four minutes down.

He continued to rake in victories with the Tour of Emilie, where once again he came home alone – and the same with the Three Valleys of Varesine.

From that time on, Bartali acknowledged publically that Coppi had become his number one adversary.

The turn of the year was unfortunately marred by sadness for the man from Piedmont. One morning, in the barracks, the postmaster handed him a telegram. He already had a premonition about its contents. His father had died on the 29th December, after dictating his last wishes to his elder brother and asking for the window to be opened so that he could look upon the countryside one last time before passing over to the next world. He wasn't even fifty.

'He was a good, strong man who was deeply attached to his land,' Fausto would say. 'He worked it tirelessly twelve hours a day and taught us with his good sense and peasant wisdom to live our lives without doing ill if we were to depend on fortune's favour.

One day he was yoking up a pair of oxen when they drew together suddenly, almost crushing him. My father took a heavy blow to the side and went into shock as a result. From that day on he, who had never had any need of a doctor, saw his health decline.'

The news hit Fausto hard. It seemed to him that his best part had taken off to where his father lay in the little cemetery of San Biagio. Domenico was not only his father but the first person to understand his ambitions, his love of the bike, and to help him as best he could.

For several weeks, the grief caused by the loss of his father left him broken and distraught. It took all his brother Livio's authority to get him to pull himself together again. But results, in that early season of 1942, were slow in coming.

Coppi and Bartali came face to face on the starting line of the one-day race for the Italian national championship in Rome on the 21stJune. Their reunion was to result in a showdown.

The race got off to a fast start. Fausto was once again the victim of implacable bad luck when after fifty kilometres he heard one of his tubs give up the ghost. And, as all help was forbidden, he had to change it himself. At the cost of a long and violent effort he managed to get back to the bunch which was going flat out, zipping along at 40 kph. But here was evidence that good form had at last returned to him after so many months of sacrifices.

A general shake-out subsequently took place. Several chasers regrouped, counter-attacking behind the two-up break of Bizzi and Ricci. Among them were Coppi and Bartali. Before long, Coppi, faithful to his old habits and feeling good, launched an offensive. Bartali couldn't hold him and fell back. Coppi rejoined Bizzi and Ricci and picked up the pace to such an extent that they soon lost Bizzi. Ricci managed to hang on until the finish but Coppi beat him in the sprint thus becoming road champion of Italy.

Bartali showed up eventually, nearly seven minutes in arrears. On learning that Coppi had just won the national title the Tuscan was visibly shaken and disorientated. He left the stadium, his shoulders suddenly weighed down as if by a heavy burden.

For all that he was national road champion, Coppi did not intend to desert the track On the 29th June, eight days after his victorious championship, he qualified for the pursuit final. Unfortunately, while he was warming up for the actual race, he crashed heavily by touching the wheel of another competitor on the bend and fractured his right collar-bone. Logically Cino Cinelli, the other finalist, should have become the national champion but he, good sport that he was, would have nothing of a title won on a walkover. He demanded that the date of the final be put off until the 9th October. Coppi was forced to convalesce for two months and ten days which was in no way prejudicial since on the appointed day he was able to catch his opponent after 4,160 m at an average speed of 48.317 kph (30mph).

With such an exploit under his belt, he set his sights on the World

Hour Record which represents the ultimate in cycling prowess. But the preparation for an hour against the clock demands intense and sustained effort.

In 1942, all Europe had settled into war and athletic feats were pushed into the background. Nevertheless Coppi decided to attack the record held at that time by the Frenchman, Maurice Archambaud, with an average speed of 45.840kph (27.5mph). But his preparation could not have been more haphazard. The chosen venue for the attempt, Milan's Vigorelli with 397.37m to the lap, was being used as a marshalling yard by the army and when by chance the track was free the aspirant record holder had to train under threat of air-raid warnings which were daily more numerous over Milan.

Nothing much was achieved in the way of back-up care either. For the big day Cavanna was only able to lay his hands on a little camphorated oil and some caffeine from a friend's pharmacy. And to crown it all, Coppi had to take to the track with a shoulder still aching from the broken collar-bone in June.

On Saturday the 7th November 1942, the day fixed for the attempt, Coppi announced to Cavanna that he had slept badly the night before but the masseur reassured him:

'You're in good shape today, Fausto. Your muscles are supple, their tone is fantastic, I can feel it.'

Stretched out on the table, taking his ease in the expert hands of his trainer, Coppi, still a little anxious, ran an eye over his schedule:

'31.4 seconds a lap adds up to 35 metres over an hour – I won't try to do any better. You know what, you'd have to be daft to take this bloke Archambaud for anything but a tough nut. I'm going to have a hell of a time this evening getting over it.'

'Relax, Fausto. Stop thinking about it. From this moment on, you've got to be a machine, a clock. All you've got to do is concentrate on pushing your 52x15. I think you've chosen well there, with the gear, neither too small nor too big. With 7.37 metres you're gaining six centimetres on Archambaud for every turn of the pedals. Your bike is a jewel: 7.500kg. A kilo less than the Frenchman's. Close your eyes, take it easy. You're going to make them really sit up: 'he did it just like that, without any special preparation.' They're not to know that you've had it in mind for quite a while. Think of the impact abroad…Oh yes, I know, but the war won't last for ever. Believe me, the Hour Record pays dividends. One day you'll travel, you'll discover France. And when the French set eyes on you, the first thing they'll say is: 'That's Coppi, the Hour Record holder.' And what about the 25,000 lira prize, you won't turn up your nose at that, to say nothing of what Legnano will come through with. Okay, lets get on that track. It's nearly two now and you ate at ten – that'll be fine. Here, have a sip of hot tea.'

It was exactly 12 minutes past 2 when Coppi took to the track in his olive green jersey. It quickly became apparent that he was totally inexperienced because he started too fast. At first he was passing the line on each lap ahead of the bell then he fell behind, a slight but worrying five seconds on the 30th lap. He was suffocating; while fighting to hold his line and maintain a rhythm, his breathing was laboured.

At the half hour he had lost ground, having covered 22,946km as against Archambaud's 23007. His progress was so gruelling to watch that no one present felt up to making any forecast. Only Emilio Colombo, a masseur, was prepared to commit himself:

'He will pull it all back in the end because he's a 'natural,' he said.

At the end of the 70th lap, hope revived. Fausto had reduced his deficit and was now within two seconds of Archambaud's record. Hope was fulfilled by the 84th when the Italian was 2.3 seconds up on the Frenchman. Four laps later, however, Fausto's margin in hand stood at only 0.6seconds.

At this point, Cavanna decided that the moment had come to cheer on his protégé. His encouragements had the effect of a whiplash. The machine found new fuel and by the 95th lap his advantage had returned to 2.3 seconds.

On the 101st lap he still hung on to a 1 second lead. He lost, then he pulled back.

Coppi was progressing in fits and starts. By digging deep inside himself he was able to scrape back a few seconds before the bell, which was a kind of examining judge in the matter. After 115 laps of the track he was getting round as best he could, no longer concerned about style, rhythm or elegance – he was suffering too much.

At the end of the 115th, he covered another 120metres, passed the pennant which denoted Archambaud's record then two seconds later the fatal bell rang. Coppi had had the time to ride another 31 metres, and that was his gain on the former summit of the sport. 31 instead of the expected 35; 45.871 to Coppi as against 45.840 for Archambaud.

The announcement of Coppi's performance was greeted with some scepticism by Maurrice Archambaud who had come into possession of photographic evidence in which there was no trace of the regulation sand bags which should line the inside of the track during an official record attempt. By such means he was pursuing the claim that Coppi had not improved upon his record.

He was a bit too quick off the mark. Nevertheless, the officials deliberated over the problem and the director of the French Cycling Federation, Colonel Beaupuis, tried to show, on a blackboard, that, in reality, Coppi had covered 45.798km (instead of 45.871) and that Archambaud 45.767 (instead of 45.840). He took into account the famous blue line drawn around the inner perimeter of the track in all velodromes which was demarcated by placing sand bags or rubber tubes during record attempts so that a rider could not go below it and thus shorten the distance travelled. His figures were the ones eventually ratified by the officials of the Union Cycliste Internationale.

Coppi's record stood for fourteen years.

*Fausto Coppi before leaving for the Tunisian front during the
1939-1945 war*

THE PRISONER OF CAPE GOOD

AT THE AGE OF TWENTY THREE, Coppi could count a Tour of Italy, national championships on road and track and the coveted title of World Hour record holder among his laurels.

The gallant old Eberardo Pavesi had seen to it that his protégé was placed under the command of a colonel who was keen on cycling and everything seemed to be in order. Unfortunately the colonel fell victim to a shake-up and was posted elsewhere so Coppi found himself under another whose idea of sport consisted of hit-and-run tactics on the battlefield.

The champion of Italy and Hour Record holder asked for no favours. Yet he wasn't short of advisers. 'You better get yourself declared unfit, otherwise they'll put you in a company going to fight in Africa,' said Giovanni Cuniolo one day – he used to be a classy rider in the pioneering age.

This valiant old pro tried to bring some influence to bear on the authorities, but was told that in wartime there were other things to do besides finding a soft option for a cycling champion. To the Italian army, Fausto was no more than number 7375 attached to the 38th infantry, Ravenna division and the new colonel's first move was to cancel all special leave until further notice.

Cavanna, for his part, seeing 'his' champion being spirited away from him advised Coppi to go sick. He could get him out of going to Africa thanks to a little 'medication' of his own; all he need do was place a Tuscan cigar, previously soaked in a special decoction, under his armpits.

But Fausto continued to assert that he didn't want to be a 'dodger'. So inevitably the worst occurred.

One day the colonel put on his full dress uniform and assembled his regiment on the parade ground. As far as he was concerned, the supreme reward was being offered them: the chance to fight a war in Africa.

In March 1943, Coppi's regiment embarked for Tunisia. As he was about to leave, Fausto, with a heavy heart, took a last look at his racing bike, the one he had used to beat the Hour Record.

At Naples, en route for Tunisia via Sicily, Cuniolo made one last effort to keep the man from Piedmont on home soil. To no avail. In the boat which was bringing him to Castelvetrano where he would catch the plane, he reflected with a great depth of sadness on the fate of the 'dodgers.' Then he was overwhelmed by a terrible nausea.

He felt himself to be alone. Just when he needed a little understanding he found all doors closed against him. Later he would remember the smile on the faces of certain 'dodgers' as they watched him leave for Africa. On his return he would hear some of these characters talking as if they had been his benefactors. He had to live with the resultant anger for a long time.

Coppi's African campaign was without doubt one of the briefest in history. As soon as they set foot in Tunis, the company was transported by lorry down south towards the Mareth line, a position established in the desert and held by the English under Montgomery with a furious barrage of firepower, despite the suffocating heat, and ably supported in the air by a force superior to that of the Italians.

' I was ill prepared for the rigours of the climate, and for the stress of battle,' Fausto would later explain, 'our regiment was decimated as much by sickness as by combat. And also, it must be said, no one had much confidence in the outcome of the war; defeat was marching towards us in seven league boots and everyone knew it.

We were all thinking of our families left behind in Italy. The radio kept us up to date on the terrible bombardments endured by the towns of the peninsula. Even if we were to save our skins in that hell, would it not be to find one day that our homes were in ruins and our people in mourning?

This anxiety which gripped us day in day out added to the news of successive reverses suffered by our troops – which the communiqués no longer even tried to cover up – the absence of supplies, the ravages produced by fever and dysentery, all that and more was explanation enough for Montgomery's famous light infantry, the 'Desert Rats,' to take private Coppi prisoner at Cape Good on the plain between Mateur and Medjez-el-Bab. It was the 13th April 1943.'

At the time of their surrender, he and his compatriots were only a handful of men, gaunt and in tatters, their hollowed, feverish eyes shining out from faces darkened by weeks of stubble.

'How did the whole thing happen?" Fausto was later asked. And he had to reply that he didn't even know himself.

'For the last forty eight hours," he confided to journalists, "we were cut off behind the lines. Our company commander invoked the Blessed Virgin or screamed blue murder while thumping his field telephone which had become obstinately silent. From time to time someone would empty his magazine into the air, anywhere, for no reason other than to make a bit of noise or strafe the African night with red flashes.

All at once somebody touched me on the arm:

'Don't move, Fausto! The English are here. Our war is over. We were taken prisoner.'

There then commenced a long period of detention in the desert sands and on the 17th May, Coppi was passed on to an assembly point at Medjez-el-Bab.

The guards were hardly severe and the discipline was not particularly rigid. But who would think of escaping? Lost in the middle of an ocean of sand, anyone trying would have no chance of coming through.

By good fortune, Coppi happened upon a chap from Tortona, a certain Eteocle Ventura who helped him make the best of his captivity. The two of them rapidly became good friends and Ventura, who had been confined for a year already, sought ways to console his compatriot, intimating that their life wasn't as bad as all that. With Ventura around the time seemed to pass more quickly because they were both able to swap memories and recall people that they had left behind in the countryside around Carezzano, Paderna, in Novi and Tortona.

Ventura encouraged his comrade to attend the training scheme for heavy goods drivers. He had something in mind. A heavy goods driver was a privileged person in the pecking order of the camp. It must be said that the morale of the prisoners was hardly bright and shining. One day several of his companions questioned Fausto:

'It's going from bad to worse, don't you think.'

He replied in all seriousness:

'Not for me it isn't, if you don't mind. Churchill called from London because once the war is over he wants me to take over the job of restructuring British cycling.'

Coppi was able to keep a straight face and his friends went so far as to wish him good luck.

Towards the end of January the background began to lighten. Ventura rushed up to his pal to announce that they had succeeded in being posted to the assembly depot at Blida, in Algeria.

Once there, life passed smoothly without any upset. Fausto and Ventura continued with their lorry driving. At the wheel of his cumbersome vehicle, Coppi began to make plans, dreaming of Bruna, the little Genoan that events had prevented him from marrying and who was waiting for him in Sestri Ponente. Love was his constant companion, giving him new reasons for hope and expectation. When they married they would buy a car and he sought the advice of Cuniolo who was a Fiat dealer. The future looked rosy. His cycling career had enabled him to put aside some thirty six thousand lira. Of course, he was thinking, too, of buying a house; things were fine at Castellania, but with the advent of Bruna it was necessary to contemplate living elsewhere.

But soon Fausto was to suffer a grave disillusionment. He had left all his money in the hands of his parents who, won over by Fascist propaganda and in the face of rising prices, had converted the whole amount into government bonds. Once Fausto got wind of this, he flew into a blinding rage.

Meanwhile in Blida it became known that ten lorry drivers and eight motorcyclists were going to be posted to Italy, to an RAF camp and Coppi had been chosen as one of the group.

On the 1st February 1945, he and the other seventeen selected members of the expedition boarded the 'Ville d'Oran,' which was packed to the gunwales, for an interminable crossing. Two days later, in the morning, the sun came up and Vesuvius hove into view. Naples welcomed them, a Naples still with open wounds, but Naples nevertheless, presiding over its magnificent bay. Coppi was still a captive, don't let us forget, but the mere fact of seeing his homeland after twenty agonising months summoned up emotion enough to overwhelm him – his eyes filled with tears.

The RAF camp was situated at Caserta where Coppi became batman to an officer, a certain lieutenant Trowell. This man knew nothing of cycle racing and the whole matter left him completely indifferent. But Coppi was quite happy to be a batman in Italy rather than seeing to himself in an African prison camp.

As it happened however, his fortunes were on the up and up. He met Busani who played football for Naples and they got on well. The footballer was full of admiration for the cyclist and he went as far as to pass on his enthusiasm to a local journalist, Gino Palumbo, in these terms: "I've just seen the Hour Record holder, Fausto Coppi, who is dying to let everyone know that he is alive and kicking."

With these words an extraordinary chain of events was set in motion. In Rome the 'Corriere dello Sport' picked up the story – without quoting the source – from the Naples daily 'Il Mattino' according to whom "Coppi was training like mad." Soon afterwards a plucky small lightweight manufacturer from the capital, a certain Mr Nulli, asked to see the prisoner-cum-cycling champion. Negotiations were then set in motion with the RAF with a view to Coppi riding in the Nulli colours. The occupying forces agreed to let their prisoner start in races provided that they took place in an area between Rome and the south of the country. While taking his leave of Fausto, the intrepid manufacturer slipped him twelve thousand lira in return for a temporary contract with Nulli cycles.

Fausto felt himself come back to life, even if his roommates made fun of him because of the name 'Nulli' which means 'nil' or 'nothing' in Italian.

'You're going to look a right Charlie with a nought on your back, you the World Record holder'

Coppi did not rise to the bait. Deep down he felt that the whole thing was a kind of symbol. He was starting from scratch again, the clock had been reset to zero for his second career.

'I think,' he was to acknowledge in later life, 'that I could never be grateful enough to that good-hearted artisan who restored my 'joie de vivre' under his zero trademark.'

Coppi was invited to take part in the first track meet at the Appio velodrome in Rome for which he was paid sixteen thousand lira – a sum which made him jump for joy. His state of health, on the other hand, remained precarious. He was very thin and suffering from an attack of malaria which made him fear that he would never again become the champion he once was.

"I am only a shadow of myself," he wrote to one of his friends, 'and I'm beginning to fear for the future. However, let's be patient; for the moment, all I want to do is get home.'

But Coppi was soon to realise that he had lost none of his old class. He rode a few races in southern Italy for which the only prize money came from a whip-round among the crowd. In these he took a fourth place behind Leoni, Bertocchi and L.Maggini then resumed his series of solitary victories in the Salvioni and Cabdelotti cups.

In May 1945 the war came to an end. Bit by bit, Coppi travelled up towards the north on his bicycle. Trains only ran occasionally since certain tracks were damaged. At one point he got a lift in an army lorry which was going in his direction. When he later told the story, safe home in Castellania, there could be little doubt that fate had smiled upon him that day.

"The lorry was chock-full of prisoners and internees. I found a place at the rear of the platform with my legs dangling over the tailboard. Suddenly a violent pitch threw me onto the road. When I came to, the lorry had vanished. There was nothing left of it but a tangle of scarp metal with dead bodies lying around at the bottom of a ravine two hundred metres below me."

Fausto stopped off at Carezzano to embrace his fiancee. Their marriage was fixed for the end of the year. Then he rejoined his family and went up to pay his respects at his father's grave in the San Biaggo cemetery.

Still in that troubled year, Coppi pulled off a major exploit in the Circuit of the Aces in Milan on Sunday 8th July. In front of a crowd of fifty thousand, the man who had just emerged from a long and painful period of imprisonment won at an average of over 26 mph. People could hardly believe their eyes given what the country had just been through and the difficulty of present circumstances.

The next day the sporting press was full of it: "We were introduced to a brand-new Coppi, a rider somewhat diminished physically but whose style was much more mature. His pedalling action in the final stages was superbly impressive both in its fluency and its power. Returning to Milan which he had not seen since beating the Hour Record on its 'magic track', he found his public more enthusiastic than ever."

So it was that this columnist in the 'Gazzetta dello Sport' made it seem almost normal to witness another Coppi win thus dismissing the fact of his captivity as if it had never happened. The wheel turns and life goes on.

Behind the scenes, as it were, during this period Fausto's younger brother, Serse, was trying to make a name – well at least a christian name – for himself. Serse wasn't a professional, but belonged to the lower echelon of the 'Independents.' As such he could take on the professionals. The two brothers were thus able to line up at the start of the Milan-Varzi race in the colours of the Lazio Sporting Club.

Fausto knew his brother well. He felt that he was capable of great things so on this occasion he put himself at the disposal of his amateur brother.

The race was run off at a lively pace. With sixty kilometres to go Serse decided to leave the bunch to try and rejoin a breakaway group which had been in the lead since the first few kilometres. He got up to them and then, wanting to go one better, he took off again leaving them for dead as he sailed away to a lone victory. His elder brother came in seven minutes down to take second place. Serse waited to hand him the winner's bouquet. It was a touching scene.

At the end of September, Fausto Coppi won the Lugano Grand Prix. One detail stood out from all the rest in this classic time-trial. The man from Piedmont flew round the final circuit at an average speed of twenty seven and a half mph.

On the domestic front, a new life opened up for him. He married Bruna at Sestri Ponente on the 22nd November and they went to live on the Via Omonima with the young bride's parents. The flat was by no means the height of luxury. Their bedroom overlooked a rather run-down square, but for Fausto nothing was more agreeable than this return to normal life after the hard times he had just been through.

In this old suburb of Genoa, Fausto was still suffering from malaria. Numerous bouts of fever which came one upon another at shorter and shorter intervals often kept him in bed. As a result he made ready to undergo a rigorous course of treatment based on the drug quinine.

He already knew that for 1946 he would no longer be riding in Legnano colours. The famous Bianchi firm had made eyes in his direction. He was embarking on a new stage of his career, one which would lead to a fiercer rivalry between himself and Bartali.

Two Clans

Coppi set his heart on being ready for the 19th March, the day of the 'classic' Milan- San Remo which is the traditional season opener in Italy.

From the 1st January he took up training. The Riviera climate was a great help with its abundance of sunshine and little wind. His morale should have been on the up and up, but he was uncertain of himself. He let nobody know that he was suffering from a stomach ulcer, a consequence of the malnutrition he had to endure while in captivity. He applied himself to a strict diet for fear of not being quite equal to the loftiness of his ambitions.

Little by little his fears melted away. He trained hard, starting every day by covering fifty kilometres on a fixed wheel. He built up to double the distance and in order to hit peak form he was doing two hundred kilometres a day.

Milan-San Remo came ever nearer. By now he had clocked up seven thousand training kilometres which was enough to reassure him. With the management at Bianchi he had formulated a battle-plan which would require him to attack well before the finish, at a point where the others would still be riding themselves in.

At the start he was noticeably pale. He took up a position in the front rank. Was it the debutante's nervousness which makes him take the lead as soon as the flag is dropped? Maybe. He was worried about the prime chasers, those who, thinking they had no chance of taking the prize on the Via Roma in San Remo, set their sights on the numerous primes offered by the towns en route. Fausto was anxious about this kind of individual because the bunch were never certain of seeing them again. They would pick up a prime, then two, and who could tell whether by chance they might instigate a decisive break. For this reason he decided to be on the alert.

Nearby there was a bustle around Bartali who was said to be in great form and whose merits were being trumpeted by one of his faithful lieutenants, Corrieri:

'On the Turchino, you'll see, Gino will be up there among the angels.'

The duel between Coppi and Bartali pushed all other news aside. Everyone was calculating the odds on one or the other and the press took sides. In 'La Stampa' Ruggero Radice, who signed himself 'Raro,' inclined openly towards Coppi. In his opinion the Hour Record holder would take the opportunity to score a point off his rival: "If the bunch lets him get a hundred metres up the road then he'll make San Remo with ten minutes to spare," he maintained with remarkable acuity.

The race had hardly started when someone attacked, it was the Frenchman Lucien Teisseire. This rider, from Cagnes-sur-Mer, thinking himself to be in poor physical condition and estimating that he would be unable to last very long set his sights on gleaning a few of the primes that peppered the first half of the course before sloping off for an early shower. But he wasn't alone. Four men went with him: Tarchini, Bardelli, Mutti and Barisone, and because of their company Teisseire felt obliged to pursue his effort.

Coppi chose this moment to set off on a counter attack, taking several other competitors with him. The junction was made on the plain of Lombardy. There was still two hundred and fifty kilometres to go, the Turchino pass to climb, as well as that series of testing hills known as the 'capi.'

Many pundits in the race convoy threw up their hands in dismay because it seemed such a suicidal mission, the work of men who had given up all hope of final victory. Coppi, for his part, felt perfectly at ease. His turns on the front were so punishing that they literally sapped the morale of his breakaway companions who were dropping back one by one. As soon as the first slopes of the Turchino made themselves felt, there was only one man left on his wheel, the stubborn Lucien Teisseire who was astonished to find himself still there.

His astonishment hardly had time to register when suddenly events took a brutally offensive turn with an unexpected, lightning attack from the man in the lead. There was still a hundred and forty five kilometres to go and Coppi would cover them on his own without flagging for a single instant. Not that he wasn't worried about holding out. What if his ulcer began to play up? But no, the moment passed; he took a bite to eat, all was well.

Claude Tillet, a journalist on 'l'Equipe' at the time, gave an account of this exploit and his piece took on a symbolic resonance for the immediate post-war period.

'The Turchino tunnel,' he revealed, 'was of very modest dimensions – just fifty metres long – but on the 19th March 1946 it assumed exceptional proportions in the eyes of the world. That day it was six years in length and lost in the gloom of war, for with the sudden arrival of peace, which caught everyone napping, nobody had thought to reconnect the electricity. There were reports of foreign observers mingling with the crowd of pilgrims. They waited with bated breath to see what the black hole might deliver up in the way of state secrets hitherto concealed be wartime censorship, or perhaps some firm basis for a reconciliation between peoples who had been divided for a while by the struggle.

A rumbling was heard from the depths of those six years and suddenly there appeared in the light of day an olive-greenish car stirring up a cloud of white dust.

Two policemen stood erect in the open top, as stiff as shop window dummies but for the fact that they were frantically waving their signal paddles – a sort of cake slice shape, red on one side and green on the other.

A second car threw up even more dust, and soon it was impossible to keep count. Leather clad motorcyclists – with dark eyes so large they could be mistaken for something on four wheels – filed by like children entering a fairground stall on the heels of their elders. After a while the din gave way to silence. And one last car emerged from the tunnel proceeding with majestic slowness, a wine coloured vehicle catching the watchers unawares and disconcerting them with its odd apparel.

The trunk of a man with articulated arms poked through the roof, ordering the pilgrims to clear the way ahead. This trunk had a fore- and a sur- name: Guiseppe Ambrosini, the pope of the Italian sect of cycling worship. A dusty grimace beneath a white cap appeared at the door below him and this grimace roared out to the assembled multitudes a magic formula which threw each recipient first into a trance and then into the paroxysm of a lion at the end of a red hot poker.

"Arriva Coppi," (Coppi is coming) the messenger announced. This revelation, which only the initiated had foreseen, took off down the valley, rebounding from rock to rock, issuing from two lips only to be sucked up at once by a Eustachian tube, leaving the wine coloured car with its human trunk and its white faced pierrot far behind. "Arriva Coppi! Arriva Coppi!" the hubbub sped on, with the accent firmly on the first vowel of the name.

And Coppi arrived, very quickly, as it turned out; much too quickly, in fact, for the liking of the photographers. His legs were slender and inordinately long, the torso short with the head buried between the shoulders, his eyes were rather protruding and his mouth open, searching for air – the whole paradoxically more harmonious than any one part might suggest. A 'heron' sporting Italian colours, perched high on an invisible saddle, had shaken off all the competition. His features, frozen into indifference, betrayed more boredom than effort, more resignation than enthusiasm. This strange cavalier came and went almost immediately, swallowed up by a fold in the mountainside, a bizarre silhouette like that of the celebrated get-up imagined by Cervantes four centuries earlier whose rider was also "of a robust constitution, lean of build and gaunt of countenance.'

Fausto started the descent with several minutes in hand, surrounded by an armada of following vehicles. He stormed through the town of Voltri and took to that narrow road, dotted with level crossings, which hugs the Riviera coastline up to San Remo. The Italian champion's progress was absolutely straight and true, he was undeniable. With each kilometre the gap between this mechanised athlete, whose legs pumped away like an automaton's, and his wretched adversaries widened. By dint of a stout holding operation over more than four hours, Lucien Teisseire managed to hang on to his second place but when he found his way onto the Via Roma his deficit on Coppi had risen to fourteen minutes. Ricci and Bartali came in next, the latter immediately calling for the winner's name.

'Coppi, a quarter of an hour up on the Frenchman and twenty four minutes ahead of the rest,' he was told.

There was no longer any room for doubt, Italy was split down the middle between Coppi-ists and Bartali-ites.

At the finish, delirium reigned. But as he crossed the line, Coppi didn't make the proper gestures, he had yet to learn the protocol for such occasions. He didn't throw up his arm. He kept his blue and white hat pulled down over his head. Large goggles obscured half of his face. The public took a dim view of such awkwardness.

Bartali found it hard to come to terms with so telling a defeat and the subsequent publicity surrounding his rival's exploit got on his nerves. He was on the look out for revenge.

On the 5th May, the two Italian stars showed up for the Championship of Zurich. That day, however, Coppi and Bartali came to an arrangement. Sharing the lead, having shaken off all their rivals, Bartali – who was in less than brilliant form whereas Coppi kept coming through with forceful turns on the front – promised not to contest the sprint. As it happened, the outcome was completely different. With the finishing banner in sight, Coppi marked time for a while in order to tighten his toe straps and Bartali jumped away under his nose to take the victory. Later, in order to justify himself, he maintained that he hadn't done anything out of the ordinary, merely taking the lead and Coppi was unable to keep up.

War was officially declared between the two adversaries.

A day or two later found the man from Piedmont romping home winner of the Tour of Romagna. Entering the old track at Lugo with twenty metres lead, he held off Vito Ortelli and wiped away the affront inflicted by Bartali who failed to finish what was a very demanding race.

It was no longer possible to consider the Tour of Italy as anything but a duel with daggers drawn between Coppi and Bartali.

The first named continued to suffer with his stomach. He had to take care of himself but let on to nobody.

On the fifth stage between Prato and Bologna, he crashed on the descent of the Poretta pass after crossing swords with his rival on the climb. He got back into the race and the two contestants entered the Bologna velodrome together. Coppi came out the winner by taking the sprint.

One would have thought that the Bianchi rider had well and truly gained the upper hand, but could he hold on? Besides his stomach upset – still there in the background – he was feeling the after-effects of his crash. The diagnosis was a fractured rib. This was certainly not the moment to falter, for what was coming up but the ninth stage, Chieti - Naples, which took in the climb of the Macerone pass.

Once again Coppi was dogged by bad luck. Mechanical trouble forced him to do roadside repairs, pliers in hand. All of which gave his rivals, with Bartali at the head of affairs, the impetus to attack. The man from Piedmont had only his courage to call upon. At the summit of the Macerone, he was down by more than four minutes. On the descent he tried to make up some of the deficit, but the gap remained unchanged at the finish. Although he was exhausted and feverish, his face as pale as a cadaver, he still confided to his immediate circle his determination to continue this calvary.

On the twelfth day of racing, he asked to see Doctor Campi who subsequently became his personal physician. This good man's diagnosis was hardly reassuring. There was even the recommendation that he should abandon.

Our champion, however, paid heed only to his courage. Just to show that he was still capable of mixing it with the best, he attacked and broke clear over the summit of the 'wall' of Muraglione with two minutes in hand over his rivals. But it was only a show of strength. He duly fell back into line, quite aware that, for the time being, he had to husband his forces with a view to the battle of the Dolomites which would begin between Udine and Auronzo. On that day the sickly hero seemed to shake off his illness on the slopes of the Mauria pass but Bartali, ever watchful, went with him. Side by side, they placed the Tour of Italy beyond the reach of any other contestant. Coppi took the stage and Bartali put on the pink jersey. These skirmishes were only the preliminary shots of the great battle to be fought out on the switchbacks of the Falzarego which dominates the ski-resort of Cortina d'Ampezza from its height of two thousand one hundred and seventeen metres. Fausto, ever faithful to his usual tactics, broke away. In his flowing style he towed Bartali along, but giving him no time to catch his breath – quite the reverse, in fact – he accelerated again and the Tuscan was dropped. For Coppi a lone ride lay ahead. The finish was far distant, there were still a hundred and fifty kilometres to cover. He hardly gave them a second thought. Thus with thirty five kilometres to go his lead over Bartali amounted to five minutes. He was virtual leader of the race. Something had to happen. Suddenly, up from behind, comes Bartali's old friend Aldo Bini, a Tuscan like himself, who began doing powerful turns on the front. With two against one the struggle became unequal and Coppi, though he won in the velodrome at Bassano del Grappa, was left with little over a minute in hand over Gino. It was not enough. The daily 'Tuttosport' nevertheless ran a banner headline: "Yesterday's stage belongs to one man: Fausto Coppi. Alone on the Falzarego, alone at the finish."

There was only one more stage hard enough to allow him to win the race: Bassano - Trente, the third act of the great drama of the Dolomites. He didn't have a lot of faith in his chances but for all that he put in a big effort over the Rolle pass. His misgivings were shown to be well founded. The terrain was not demanding enough and Bartali was able to stick with him. But the balance shifted once again with thirty kilometres to go. Bartali fell victim to a puncture. No favours were about to be granted the old Tuscan, the harsh law of racing would apply. Coppi jumped away, taking the useful Ronconi along with him. At the finish the countdown began. A minute had already elapsed since Coppi crossed the line and Bartali was only two minutes and fifty seconds ahead of him. Would Coppi take the pink jersey?

No, for a shout went up, a roar; Bartali came home, his face powdered with dust – and furious. He kept his trophy by forty seven seconds, Coppi was second.

From that moment the Tour of Italy was generally adjudged to be over. At the age of thirty two, Bartali had won his third national Tour. Carried in triumph by his supporters, he found himself declaring:

'Fausto has his eye on me, for the moment I've been let off, but I will never give in.'

The World Pursuit Championship in 1947

The Test of the Parisians

Fausto Coppi's reputation very quickly spilled over the frontiers from Italy. Paris wanted to make his acquaintance so he was happy to participate on the Trocado Criterium - pompously baptised 'World Trophy' - which would serve as a prelude to the Grand Prix des Nations which was run against the watch as a time-trial.

The clock at the Gare de Lyon in Paris was showing 8.40 when Fausto Coppi, accompanied by both his team manager and mechanic, first set foot on Parisian soil. At the time the press noted that he wore a shiny suit, that had obviously had much use and that his trousers fitted badly. On his head was a beret; in his hand a suitcase while smoked glasses rested on his nose. A photographer pushed himself forward, provoking the curiosity of a young girl:

"Who is it?

'Fausto Coppi, the champion cyclist.'

'You'd think it was a peasant in his Sunday suit.'

This reaction was fairly close to that of Guillaume Driessens who mixed in cycling circles, lending his services as soigneur before coming a team manager. It was Coppi's Italian masseur who asked him to look after Fausto.

'On the day, as Driessens related, we had arranged to identify each other by a pink coloured newspaper being held in his hand. Actually I saw a painfully thin boy get out of a third class carriage. His face was pale and he had a raw-boned silhouette, the cardboard suitcase he was carrying was of such poor quality that it made me doubt whether he could possibly be what the Italians already considered to be the successor to their Girardengo or Binda. However there was no doubt, it was indeed Coppi.'

The next day at the start of the criterium, he announced his intentions:

'It's the first time I've ever raced in France and I've come here to win!'

At the time his adversaries did not take this menace seriously. After a lap of honour during which he was greeted with an explosion of enthusiasm, he went off like a rocket as soon as the flag was dropped. By the sixth lap at the ten kilometre point he had taken a lead of thirty meters over the bunch containing eleven specially selected riders. Behind him all of them said good-bye to victory and on top of defeat the competitors were to be submitted to the humiliation of being lapped - except for Gino Bartali - at the end of one hundred kilometres. The Tuscan finished second, the little Henry Aubry, the recent World Amateur champion, won the bunch sprint in front of Thietard, Knecht, Piot and Wagner.

Even more astonishing was his victory three days later in the classic Grand Prix des Nations time trial when he beat Emile Idee and then a little later when he won the competitive Circuit of Lugano.

He had another important rendez-vous: the Tour of Lombardy. He rode it in his usual manner. He took the initiative alone on the slopes of the Madonna del Ghisallo. Caught by two other riders on the descent, he dropped them near the outskirts of Milan to finish alone at the Vigorelli Velodrome. There was delirium in the packed stands.

The road season was over, but Coppi did not seem satisfied. He returned to Paris to devote himself to the track where he was very successful in many events, but in particular the pursuit races.

His wife Bruna accompanied him and both of them were well received. On one occasion Bruna appeared to be slightly embarrassed when they were present at a performance at the 'Folies Bergeres' where some of the exotic dancers were a little...daring.

Alternating between road training and track racing, the road season was suddenly on them. In 1947, the newspapers did not hesitate to feed the Coppi-Bartali controversy. The public joined in. The two antagonists were summoned to explain their position. Fausto declared:

'Can I let Gino collect all the victories, parade himself everywhere in his armour of invincibility when I too feel I have the making of a champion? No, we must play the game and let the best man win... I have tried and I will try right up to my last stroke of the pedal to be the best!'

Unfortunately what followed was that Fausto and Gino both employed tactics which were fatal to both of them. Being so busy watching each other they were both to lose important events, their motto being 'Better to lose together than to see the other win!'

The hearts of the partisans of the two camps were filled with joy. The two champions eclipsed all the other Italian stars. At the stage finishes in the Tour of Italy an incredible scenario presented itself: two brigades of police specially armed with truncheons, one for the partisans of Bartali and the other for the partisans of Coppi were charged with protecting the two men from the collective enthusiasm once the finishing line was crossed. The barriers broke under the pressure of the crowd, their hotels, in spite of the intervention of the guardians of the peace, were under siege.

The press dwelt only on the rivalry between the two men. On the day after a race you could read 'Bartali beaten by Coppi' even if one finished 30th and the other 32nd. The name of the winner of the event was seemingly of little interest and written at the bottom of the page in small letters.

At the start of the 1947 season Bartali, five years older than Coppi was not afraid to affirm: 'I have never bowed at the knee before Coppi and I preserve the right to consider myself to be his equal in all circumstances!'

A sort of 'spy mania' also arose between the two men, especially on Bartali's side. The man from Tuscany had men permanently posted around Fausto to determine his morale and state of mind. The latter was in no way duped and many times was the author of false rumours which he deliberately circulated in order to alarm Bartali.

The rivalry gave birth to tactics which were meant to neutralise each other. Fausto himself, in order to prepare for an offensive and to avoid Bartali taking the initiative, lined his men up at the head of the bunch to force the pace and when he arrived at his chosen spot, launched his attack.

But Bartali was cunning. For him all was fair in love and war. Later, in the Tour of Italy 1948, he would have recourse to an astonishing stratagem to beat him on one of the stages. Gino had in fact been observing Fausto for a long time looking for a weak point where he would be vulnerable. Suddenly he thought that he had found it: a vein scarcely visible behind his right knee, swelled up when muscular fatigue was approaching. Bartali decided to profit from this discovery. When he thought it was time to take action, he delegated Giovanni Corrieri, one of his faithful team mates, to follow Coppi's wheel, with his eyes fixed on his right leg. The kilometres went by and Coppi did not weaken, continuing to ride with his unique supple pedalling action. Suddenly Corrieri let out a cry:

'The vein'

The vein had in fact swollen up. In the bunch they looked at each other inquisitively. What had happened to their Giovannino?

'The vein! The vein!;

Bartali and his men launched an attack and the man from Florence won the stage.

The fervour and piety of Gino were well known, a member of the Catholic Action Group, a brother of the Third Order of Carmelites. A Catholic to the point of fanaticism, he was willing to present himself as a mystic and he was known as 'Gino the Pious'. When he won they said that his victory had been sent from heaven. Some children even claimed one day that they had seen two angels pushing Gino up a steep hill. This showed just how far children's imagination could be influenced.

Coppi was seen as wearing a very different halo, that of the devil, a sort of materialist, an ardent defender of atheism. Put in a different way he was a man of the extreme left bitterly committed to the downfall of a holy man.

'It's true replied Fausto that I've never made the sign of the cross in public before the start of the race, I have never publicly professed my faith. However, I have been to church perhaps more times than those who belong to Catholic Action. I have even given my winner's jerseys to some of the churches and I have given them by conviction and not by way of an exhibition. In Italy, unfortunately one goes by appearances, you have to know how to lie. Having said that I do not believe in miracles in sport. The good Lord certainly has other things to do than to concern himself with the gearing on our bicycles!'

In this year of 1947, Coppi was received by the Pope Plus XII. Bartali accompanied him. Fausto many times recounted the story of the interview:

'A footman dressed in red velvet led us through the corridors of the Vatican where the carpet muffled our footsteps. It was quiet as the grave.

The Pope received us at 11 o'clock precisely, in a very simple room, which contrasted with the luxurious apartments which we had passed through beforehand. Very pale, he was seated in the full daylight behind a desk covered with books and documents and surmounted by a large silver crucifix. He spoke to us with kindness and called us his 'dear sons' and congratulated us on our success. Then with his fine translucent hand, he traced before our bowed foreheads the sign of the blessing for us and our families.'

As soon as the cycling competitions started the implacable rivalry was always there, intense and intrusive and the image of the pious Gino opposed to the materialistic Coppi, haunted many people's spirits. Curzio Malaparte was one of them:

'Bartali', he wrote, 'belongs to those whose believes in the traditions and their immutability to those who accept dogma. He is a metaphysical man protected by the saints. Coppi has nobody in heaven to take care of him. His manager, his masseur have no wings. He is alone, alone on his bicycle. He does not pedal with an angel perched on his right shoulder. Bartali prays while he is pedalling. The rational, Cartesian and sceptical Coppi is filled with doubts, he believes only in the motor that has been given to him: which is to say his body.'

And the struggle recommenced. Bartali won the first duel by taking Milan-San Remo, while Coppi replied with the Tour of Romagne where he beat his rival in the sprint.

At the start of the Tour of Italy, amid an explosive atmosphere Bartali announced:

'To win, Coppi will have to cross over my dead body!'

In the first part of the event, Coppi won the stages to Prato and Naples but Bartali won the leader's jersey. The man from Piedmont said that his victory would be established at the traditional rendez-vous in the Dolomites. He achieved it by dominating the mountains of Falzarego and of Pordi with his great class. The Tour of Italy was won for the second time.

Insatiable, eight days after bringing back the pink jersey to Milan, Coppi took the national pursuit title by beating Vito Ortelli in the final at an average speed of nearly 48kph.

In the Tour of Switzerland he won the time-trial stage and then went on to the Tour of Veneto which he took by eight minutes from Magni after a lone break of 170 kilometres. His Italian coronation came in the Coppa Bernocchi which he won again and this permitted him, with the addition of points in other Italian events, to put on a new national jersey: that of Italian Road Champion.

He returned to the track to take the World Pursuit Championship. The quality of his opponents was beyond doubt; beating Antonio Bevilcqua and Hugo Koblet into second and third places. The success was also the start of some great battles with Dutch star Geerit Schulte who was to beat Coppi in the final following year, after the Italian had beaten him easily in the semi-final on his way to the gold medal.

For his return to the road he chose 'Across Lausanne' which for him was no more than a formality in spite of the stubborn opposition of Jean Robic. In the Tour of Emile he left everyone 170 kilometres from the finish. He crossed the summit of the Abetoe with a lead of more than four minutes over Bartali and Martini who were chasing him. On the Col of the Barigazzo he had increased his advantage to seven minutes. Aroused by an indescribable enthusiasm, he arrived at the finish with more than ten minutes advance over his old rival.

The journalists were out of breath trying to find superlatives. It was difficult to describe such a superb athlete!

And it went on. In the Tour of Lombardy he once again mastered Bartali and all the others but this time also the rain, the mud and the wind. Finally he brought his 1947 season to a close by a magnificent success in Paris in the Grand Prix des Nations time trial for the second year in succession.

Fausto was happy. He was fulfilled, adored and adulated.

On the 1st November Bruna Coppi gave birth to a daughter. She was to be called Marina. Fausto would have preferred a boy. 'That will be next time' Coppi told his friends.

He really deserved a few days holiday. But the champion was much sought after. From 29th November to the 8th February he participated in an impressive series of twenty one pursuit races without ever once being beaten. Notably he was victorious over Van Steenbergen, Blanchet, Peeters, Middlekamp, Piel and Koblet...

He raced at Brussels, at Ghent, at Antwerp, at Paris, at Nice...

The winter Velodrome at Paris - the famous Vel d'Hiv - saw some remarkable performances from the Italian star.

The public who had already caught sight of Coppi came to adopt him permanently and the Coppi époque was born at the velodrome on the Boulevard de Grenelle. The fans were not mistaken, they knew an exceptional champion when they saw one. Every time on the day of the competitions, from ten o'clock in the morning, several hundreds of spectators lined up on the pavement waiting for the ticket office to open for the evening races, for none could deny Coppi's concern to satisfy the public.

What a lot of special memories there were for the spectators of these wonderful France-Italy events which traditionally took place during the month of November. In 1949 and 1950 more than 17,000 tickets were sold for some of the events and the record would be broken on the 4th November 1951 with 19,700 people paying the entry fee. So cycling beat boxing which had one time attracted 17,500 spectators for the match between Robinson and Villemain.

But let us return to the 1948 season. The curtain was lifted on the 14th March. Coppi decided to go to provoke the Belgians on their home ground at the Circuit Het Volk; a hard race made selective by the interrupted succession of cobbles and bad cycle paths. Arriving on the scene several days before the race, he went over the last twenty kilometres of the course at least twenty times and as the finish was on a track he trained there as well, minutely analysing every detail and notably the entrance to the stadium.

Fausto Coppi's presence imposed an elevated rhythm on the event. The Italian, always very well placed, commanded all the attempts to escape. Twice he was the victim of a puncture and each time he rejoined the bunch with the greatest of ease.

What could you do against such a man? Once again victory smiled on him. He won by K.O. Coppi was unique.

But after the finish he learned that he had been disqualified for an illegal wheel change. What happened? The rules stated that only riders in the same team could give aid and assistance. When the Italian punctured the first time he received a wheel from his team mate Oreste Conte. On the other hand after his second flat tyre no other Italian was able to help him. It was then that the Belgian rider Walschott spontaneously came to his aid. The rules were quite clear: illicit help meant disqualification.

The organisers struck by Coppi's crushing superiority did not disqualify him from the race but gave him second place instead.

However, Fausto would not accept this.

'If I committed a fault, he declared, I should be disqualified pure and simple. I will not accept this second place. The race was incredibly hard - possibly the most difficult I have ever contested. The cobbles made me suffer like a martyr, but I wanted to win. That's why I was obliged to make incessant efforts, to be near the head of the bunch even though this position prevented me from receiving shelter provided by the other riders. With regards to the races in Italy or France there are at least several less intense periods; whereas this was almost a continual sprint for 240 kilometres. I won but I finished very tired and these efforts will perhaps be prejudicial for me in Milan-San Remo.'

In Italy another task was waiting for him. He wanted, to nobody's astonishment, to put Bartali in his place. The rivalry was exacerbated by a sports magazine report outlining that from now on he and Fausto would share all the races between them.

'He and his cronies', raged Coppi, 'have managed to get the two time trial stages in the Tour of Italy shortened and modified because they are all afraid of me. This is not a surprising gesture...'

So, forty kilometres from the finish, Coppi dropped the last member of the break Vittorio Rossello and finishing alone added a new jewel to his crown. The second man was at five minutes, the first peloton at ten minutes and Bartali at eleven.

In this year of 1948 the Coppi-Bartali duel was scarcely to Fausto's advantage as he was literally swindled in the Tour of Italy. Winner of two mountain stages in the Dolomite he rebelled against the method Fiorenzo Magni used to preserve his leaders jersey. The rider from Monza was a very poor climber but was pushed, in the most outrageous fashion, up the hills by supporters placed every twenty meters for that very purpose. Coppi insisted that it was a scandal and decided by way of protest to retire from the Giro. His prestige was weakened. Much more than that of Bartali who, profiting from the absence of his rival went on to win the Tour de France for a second time, ten years after his first triumph.

The photo that Coppi dedicated to the future 'white lady' at the 'Three Varasian Valleys'

For An Autograph

THE YEAR 1948 WAS RATHER COLOURLESS FOR COPPI, it marked the debut of a passion which going to tear families apart and finally split the whole of Italy.

The story of the person who came to be called the 'White Lady' deserves to be held back for a few pages before trying to define the personality of this woman who opposed everybody - including the judiciary - with a rare determination before finally seeing love triumph.

She was called Giulia Occhini. Originally from Naples she came from a middle class family. At 22 years of age she had taken refuge along with her family in a little village in the province of the Marches, near to Ancona. The war was not over yet but the outcome could be forecast.

Giulia was strikingly beautiful with thick chestnut hair divided up into enormous plaits. Like the rest of the population she watched the troops pass through, the English, the Canadians and the Indians of the 8th Army as well as the Italian Regiments. Then when the front was established on the Adriatic at Rimini, a detachment of the Liberation Corps was stationed for a while in the region. In the midst of this detachment the medical section was commanded by a captain: the doctor Enrico Locatelli, a solid mature and competent man. When Giulia made his acquaintance she never dreamt that she would one day become his wife. But in those mad times everything happened very quickly.

One day when they came face to face for the second or third time, Dr Locatelli who was feeling the beginnings of a mad love for this pretty Neapolitan with fiery eyes said:

'If someone like me, older than you asked you unexpectedly to give up everything for him, how would you reply?'

What was going through the head of the young girl? Was she flustered by the uniform? By the position of a military doctor? By the bearing and the determination of the man? She seemed embarrassed and replied laughingly:

'I believe that I would say nothing. If such a thing happened to me

I would leave...'

And they got married a fortnight later, after the banns had been hastily read and an oath taken.

Dr Enrico Locatelli was a good practitioner working in difficult conditions with reduced resources due to wartime shortages. He saved and healed the maximum possible number of men. But he was not young enough to set up shop in a big town or even go further in his profession.

After settling down on the Adriatic coast the newly married couple had already known the joy of cradling their first child. Loretta was born in 1946, a little girl with a fine and perfect head. She had so much hair that her mother had to comb it straight away with a capricious little fringe on her forehead. For her mother Loretta quickly became Lolli and she was still very small when the family arrived at Varano Borghi.

Once in the locality Mrs Locatelli tried to help her husband as best as she could by trying to create a peaceful home without any worries.

She was often completely alone with Lolli. The doctor had to care for seven thousand people, men, women, children and old people.

His day began early in the morning and ended late at night.

Whenever his wife saw him at home he was always wearing his nightcoat.

When he left her it was to visit the sick in their little houses lost in the snows of Varesotto but at home he would stretch out on the sofa and open the pages of the newspaper 'Gazzetto Dello Sport'.

Yet, Enrico Locatelli was a closed and bitter man, he spoke with a rough and even brutal manner when things were not to his liking. He was authoritarian with everyone including his wife.

At Varano the couple had no friends. There was a local cinema but the best films, when they came at all did so considerably late.

Dr Locatelli's only distraction was sport in general and cycling in particular. Moreover the only racing cyclist who he really esteemed was called Fausto Coppi.

'I can picture him now during our evenings at Varano Borghi, Giulia related. I would be sitting in the corner with a big ball of wool with needles or a hook making something which always had to be finished quickly.

He would be in the armchair with a soft light behind him holding the pink pages of the Gazzetta dello Sport.

He made himself comfortable and glanced at the first page. If he found an article on Coppi, or something new on Coppi, he stopped to read it; otherwise he leafed through the newspaper until he came across something on the champion.

The rest did not interest him.

If there was nothing on Coppi - which could sometimes happen - he threw down the paper and went to bed.'

Cycling, on the other hand, left Giulia Locatelli indifferent:

'This Coppi, she surprisingly said, this Coppi, people cannot have very much else to think about if they feel so strongly about him.'

The great Coppi-Bartali reunion took place on the 8th August 1948, in the Varese area, close to the house of the Locatellis, at a big race known as The Three Valleys Varesines and Dr Enrico wanted at all cost to see the race.

'Giulia, he said to his wife, we can go there on Saturday to the race headquarters, each rider appears in person to pick up his number. So we'll be able to get quite close to Coppi.'

The prospect of such a thing hardly enchanted the young woman; but then on the other hand at least it was a chance to get out of the ghetto of Varano where the atmosphere could be sometimes oppressive.

They arrived at Varese when around fifty riders had already signed the control sheet.

Everyone was waiting for the stars.

Suddenly their car was caught up in a massive traffic jam and they found themselves directly behind a grey Lancia Aprillia with an Alessandria number plate. At the wheel was Fausto Coppi.

The couple managed to follow the car right up to the race headquarters itself, where the confusion was indescribable. Hordes of young men held on to the cars, screaming and holding onto the body work.

The Aprilia stayed with its doors tightly closed until the police arrived to disperse all the fans. But this was impossible, all they could do was push them back a little. Then - but only then - one of the doors opened and a tall sunburnt young man, very elegant, dressed in brown and wearing a blue tie, jumped out of it. It was Fausto Coppi himself.

What was going through Giulia's head? Without any apparent reason here she was playing the role of the most ardent supporter, gesticulating and shouting like everyone else, encouraging him and arguing with those around her.

'I want his autograph she shouted to her husband'. However that evening it was quite impossible to get close to Coppi. The couple agreed to come back the next day to see the race and to salute the star after the finish. An explosive atmosphere reigned over the start of the event, where the 'Coppists' and the 'Bartalists' threw insults at each other. The race would also serve as some sort of pointer for the forthcoming World Championships, yet another reason to reinforce the rivalry between the two men. Coppi was unlucky in the early part of the race. Half-way round the first lap he was the victim of a crash and with a painful arm he was five minutes down on the bunch. His fragile morale could only add to the disappointment.

Quickly, Tragella his team manager helped him back on his machine but inside Fausto ' the spring was broken'.

'I'm stopping, it's hurting too much'.

'It's nothing Fausto', Tragella replied, 'the race has only just started. You can get back. You'll see. Go on, you've nothingto lose.'

So he continued on his way forgetting all his suffering. Soon a mad rage came over him. he saw only one goal; to catch Bartali. With his team mates who had waited for him, he went so fast that he broke the lap record. But the bunch were not dawdling, for the chase was being organised to bring back the four riders who had escaped, as well as preventing Coppi from rejoining. The loudspeaker gave the names of the men in the break, they were; Tonio Bevilacqua, Luciano Maggini, Vito Ortelli and Luciano Pezzi. For Fausto he first had to catch the peloton. After that, one would see. The gap between the pack and him was reduced. His effort was so violent that some of his own men lost contact. At the half-way point of the race Coppi was finally back into the peloton and refound....Bartali. Soon the escapees themselves were brought to heel. The finish was close. The crowd had eyes only for Coppi and Bartali. A group of ten rides approached the finishing line and Bartali started the sprint. Giulia remembers that day the cries of the commentator who screamed; Bartali, 'Bartali, Bartali,' then a second's silence...'Winner Coppi.'

Everything happened so quickly but she was able to see Coppi, who smiled and raised his arm for a victory salute. Dr Locatelli's wife was enraptured. More than ever she wanted the winner's autograph. She shouted to one of his entourage, Giovanni Chiesa, one of the champion's most trusted men, while Coppi was already back at his hotel. 'Do you think I can get close to Fausto to ask him for a signed photo? The trusty Chiesa was doubtful.

' Madame, you saw him. He's injured. At the moment he will be in his bath and then he'll be on the massage table. And you know we have our orders. We've been told to let nobody pass. So...'

But Giulia insisted. Chiesa, in order to have a clear conscience went to Coppi and said to him,

'Faustino ! There's a couple here; a Doctor and his wife. She wants a souvenir from you, a photo, an autograph or something.....

' At this hour? replied Fausto, when I'm being treated and so many things to do ?'

'You're not obliged to Fausto...'

Coppi thought for a moment and then said to his friend.

' OK. Go and tell them I'll be down in half an hour.'

Thirty minutes later Coppi found himself in front of the couple. The Doctor had led his wife stay a few feet in front of him and it was she who rushed forward to meet the champion.

' I'd like an autograph, please? An autograph and a photo.'

'Give me a photo,' he asked his brother Serse. Then turning towards the Doctor's wife, 'Well, we'll write 'with friendship to ....?'

'Giulia!'

And Fausto at last held out what had been demanded of him; a postcard with him wearing the Italian Champion's jersey. He appeared to be very young with an expression that was all his own; smiling but melancholic.

It was the first meeting between Giulia and Fausto who quickly forgot the young woman, preoccupied as he was by the end of the season. In actual fact his problems were far from over.

The Coppi-Bartali rivalry reached its zenith a few days later at Valkenburg in Holland, during the World Championship on the road. The two antagonists marked each other, neutralised each other and accumulated such a deficit that both of them retired. The Italian Cycling Union was so deeply shocked by this negative attitude when wearing the national colours that the verdict they gave was a severe one : two months suspension for each of them with the following reprimand :

'In the professional World Championships on the road, they forgot the honour that was granted to them to uphold Italian prestige. Thinking only of their personal rivalry they abandoned the competition, arousing the unanimous reprobation of all sportsmen.'

Two months of penitence would not alter Coppi's physical form but on the contrary increased his thirst for glory. Besides success in the Tour of Emile, it was the Tour of Lombardy that he was aiming for. In this event he relied purely on his strength. On the climb of the Madonna del Ghisallo, he literally flew away to beat the record for the climb. His solitary adventure lasted for eighty kilometres and he relegated all his pursuers to nearly five minutes as he crossed the finishing line. At the end of the 1948 season, Coppi had only great objective for the next season: to win the Tour de France.

Towards the Absolute.

In 1949 everything began with the Milan-San Remo which was won by Fausto Coppi. Where, oh where were the journalists going to find the words powerful enough to reflect their feelings. The Frenchman Edouard Fachlietner was the first to actively show himself in this 'Classic'. Behind him were Magni, Ortelli, Rossello, Leoni and Kubler. Coppi chose to mount his attack on the Capo Berta. Exactly as planned, he produced a furious effort. On the climb he passed all those who were counter-attacking and caught the unfortunate Frenchman just before the summit. Then he launched himself into the descent towards Imperia and arrived in triumph at San-Remo. In less than thirty kilometres he managed to put four minutes into his rivals.

Alongside him, his brother Serse was pursuing, with less vivacity of course, the career of a roadman, never hesitating to give his brother all the help of which he was capable. He even managed to win the Paris-Roubaix after an 'armchair' ride. Victory had smiled on the robust Breton Andre Mahe who had broken away from the bunch. But he was misdirected at the entrance to the velodrome and classified equal first with Serse Coppi, winner of the sprint of a small group which arrived a few minutes later.

Fausto, himself, came up with the unexpected: a pursuit match at the Vigorelli against Geerit Schulte. The Italian had got his revenge over the Dutchman after the World Championships in 1948 and the two men were now equal, so this event would be the decider. Their rivalry filled several columns in the newspapers and on the 10th April the Vigorelli track at Milan was bursting at the seams. Fausto felt nervous. After the first lap he was two metres up. On the second lap the two champions were level; on the third Schulte led by a wheel. At this stage it would be better to let Coppi himself describe what transpired:

'The nervous tension which had never left me made my legs tight and affected my breathing. Inexorably, Schulte started to gain ground; each lap his lead went up. The crowd was screaming to encourage me, then went quiet when my defeat seemed certain. For two laps I had the

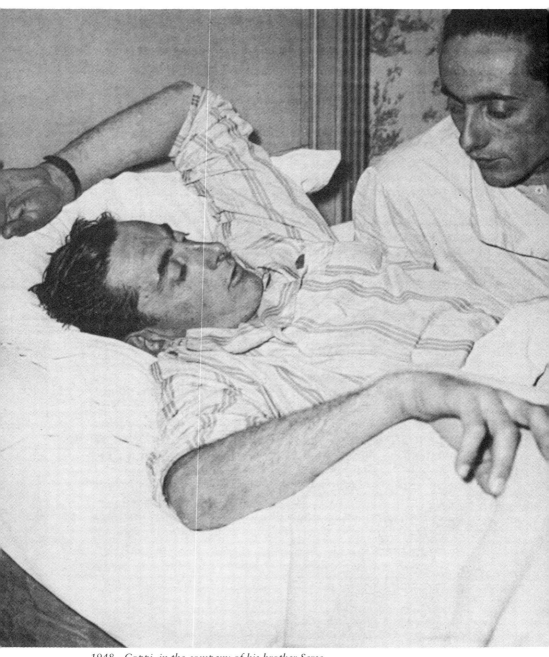

1948 - Coppi, in the company of his brother Serse.
An understanding of unparalleled complicity

impression of riding through a long desert. All I could hear was the noise of the wheels on the wooden track and my panting for breath. My legs just did not want to turn. There was nothing that could be done. I felt bound up hand and foot, shrivelled up like a piece of dead wood. With three laps to go I got the impression that Schulte was beginning to tire, his lead had come down a bit. Then in the last desperate effort I pressed harder on the pedals. During the penultimate lap Schulte had an advantage of two metres. On the last lap we were level. Then something happened which I will never forget. The public who had been quiet with disappointment, already resigned to my defeat, exploded. As one, 20,000 people got to their feet and screamed my name, louder and louder, chanting and chanting as the seconds ticked by and the finish approached. I was completely extended by nervous tension and exhaustion but the repeated cry suddenly gave me superhuman strength. I continued to turn the pedals like an automation and reached the end with a four metres lead : six tenths of a second.'

Coppi willingly admitted that these pursuit races on the track were in his opinion the most exhausting of all, that they left him broken and he had difficulty in regaining his nervous and physical equilibrium. It was however somewhat difficult to believe, for three days after this extraordinary duel he lined up at the start of the Flèche Wallonne with an astonishing physical form. He was going to prove the Belgian roadmen on their home ground and notably the celebrated Rik Van Steenbergen.

With approximately one hundred kilometres to go, Coppi thrust himself to the front and went clear of the pack....only a single rider was able to resist him: Pino Cerami. The victorious arrival of the two men was being predicted when three other adversaries surged up from behind, one of which was the famous Rick Van Steenbergen. The latter had a tremendous reputation as a sprinter and had no trouble of disposing of Coppi once the finishing banner was in sight. However the affair was not over. Some of the followers complained that the Belgian had only been able to get up with the complicity of some of the following cars and the result was a false one. Needless to say the dispute on Belgian soil was not settled in favour of the Italian. He returned to Italy to win the Tour of Romagne in a stunning fashion after a lone break. Bartali arrived ten minutes later.

The start of the Tour of Italy was suddenly upon them and Coppi declared that he was ready. As was his habit he showed all his brilliance when climbing over the Dolomites. He won at Bolzano (he had already won at Salerno earlier in the race) but all eyes were turned towards the purple passage of this the 32nd Tour of the Italy, the 17th stage Cuneo-Pinerolo. The route was the combined work of the race director, Vincenzo Torriani and of the 'technician' of the Tour de France, Jean

Garnault. It was in actual fact a Franco-Italian course which borrowed the French roads for the Cols de Vars, de l'Izoard, de Madeleine and du Montgenevre. After which the riders returned to Italy to once again climb the Col de Sestrières after which, there remained 55 kilometres before reaching the Pinerolo for a total distance of 254 kilometres.

Once again the riders found themselves before the spectacle of a fantastic cavalcade. Escaping on the Col de la Madeleine the transalpine champion would be alone for 190 kilometres in the rain and cold leading over the top of all the climbs. Relating the event in 'Miroir-Sprint' Albert Baker d'Isy could scarcely believe his eyes:

'Knights without armour, bare legs, bodies covered with a simple thin jersey, Fausto Coppi and Gino Bartali came to the French roads to dispute the most moving of tournaments. Passing before the Italian followers who had crossed the frontier, were some mountain troops, a few dozen Italians from France who had climbed up the valley, several mountain shepherds and a handful of privileged French journalists. In other circumstances, the absence of the public would have created what is known as 'a lack of atmosphere', an unfortunate impression of emptiness. We do not feel that those who on top of the Vars or the Izoard would have felt that. The duel, rapidly turning to Coppi's advantage, was on the contrary the finest and purest in this grandiose solitude of this day of the week, when a 'foreign Tour' went past.

Never had the 'Casse Deserte', this majestic flaw in the climb up the Izoard, deserved its name so well and the broken red obelisks of stone casting their shadows across the road seemed to salute Fausto and Gino, two men of their stature who were worthy of them. There was no third man, or at least he was of no interest to us... He was far behind. He had nothing to do with this particular duel which was quickly going Fausto Coppi's way, a simple streamlined champion who put us in mind of the pure lines of the Acropolis or the fine fuselage of a modern aeroplane.

But the most extraordinary thing was to see him make the acquaintance of the Izoard. You clearly felt that Coppi had been waiting for this moment for a very long time. Had the Izoard not done more for the glory of his rival Bartali than all the mountains in Italy put together? And it was perhaps to hasten the moment that Coppi went to the front and went away on the Col de Larche before the French frontier.

We were at the big bend that was dominated by the Queyras monument to the dead. The Col de L'Izoard seemed even to have taken root in the valley of the Guil, the happy boiling torrent. At that moment Coppi had a lead of five minutes although he had punctured five times (wheel changes were authorised) and had then taken his time to eat his food, emptying his musette in the process. He had consumed it in small but regular amounts when riding through the valley of the Queyras.

It was only then that we understood Coppi's superiority, his state of freshness and his remarkable calm. Nothing escaped him as he glanced to the left and to the right as he followed the direction arrows and the read the kilometre stones. So he made the acquaintance of this redoubtable adversary that he would return to in the Tour de France. And he seemed to say, 'Ah! it's you Mr Izoard. Enchanted to make your acquaintance. You have not got the forbidding manner that they told me about and that Gino would have me believe. We can become good friends, you know!'.

And Fausto's lead on Gino increased as he climbed round the bends of the savage mountain. In the last fifty kilometres he accelerated the pace again, which enabled him to cross the line twelve minutes before Bartali. After this testing stage, the Tour of Italy was over, the last three stages were a formality. On the final general classification, Coppi left Bartali in second place at 23'47". For the Italians Coppi became the 'Campionissimo', the champion of champions. People pressed him to ride the Tour de France. He decided to do it. Too often he had seen written on Italian roads: 'Coppi! In order to be a great champion you need the yellow jersey'.

Before the start of the great French event, lots of problems remained to be resolved because Coppi's participation remained linked to the non-selection of Bartali. He reproached the old Tuscan for his lack of team spirit, his rebelling against the most elementary rules of the game, especially during a stage race. Several meetings were necessary before he was prepared to accept Bartali in the team. The peace was at last sealed at Chiavari and confirmed a few days later at the Hotel Andreola at Milan. An official act was transcribed in which the rights and duties of both interested parties were defined. In Paris the following Italian team was presented: Bartali, Coppi, Milano, Biagoni, Brignole, De Santi, Pasquini, Pezzi, Ricci, Vincenzo Roselle and Sciardis. There were other Italians in the race, the six members of the 'Italian cadets'. Magni, Ausenda, Martini, Pedroni, Peverelli, and Cerami. Alfredo Binda, manager of the Italian national team, thought that the Alps would select the eventual winner. He did not think for a moment about the Pyrenees which would be crossed first.

On the fourth stage from Boulogne to Rouen the French team tried to show that they were a force to be reckoned with, in spite of all their weaknesses. Louison Bobet, for example did not seem to have the form of 1948. At the finish the operation did not seem so bad as the 'tricolour' Lucien Teisseire won the stage. The yellow jersey was worn by a member of a regional team; Jacques Marinelli. The day was hardly advantageous for the Italians; Coppi and Bartali were almost 18 minutes down.

At their Hotel in the centre of Rouen, there was an uneasy

atmosphere. Binda tried to be reassuring and suddenly, Coppi declared: 'Tomorrow I must be at the front.'

The next day, on the stage from Rouen to St Malo - 293 kilometres - the riders were suffering in the heat. Coppi attacked, taking with him the yellow jersey Marinelli, Kubler, Gauthier, Dussault, and several others. The lead soon went up to three minutes and then six. It was getting hotter and hotter when the escapees - at the 75th kilometre - entered the little village of Mouen in the county of Calvados. It was here that an incident took place which was to have unfortunate consequences for Coppi. It was caused by a spectator who was holding out a bottle of beer to be taken by a competitor. In her awkwardness she obstructed Marinelli and caused him to crash. Coppi could not avoid him and both fell heavily. Marinelli got up and was quickly back on his bike, but Coppi could not restart as his machine was damaged. He asked for his spare bike. This was on Binda's little Renault. But where was the team manager? His real place was behind Coppi, to give him any assistance he might need, but Binda had been held up at the feeding station at Caen. When he finally arrived, Coppi who had refused a bike from the assistant team manager, took his own spare machine. But his heart was no longer in it. What had happened to him? Hunger, thirst, anger or disappointment. He was making little progress. Binda implored him, exhorted him, called on his pride. Nothing could be done. Fausto was pedalling at the speed of a postman..... or almost.

When he crossed the finishing line, 18'40" had ticked by since the arrival of the Swiss Ferdi Kubler. On general classification he occupied 25th place nearly 37 minutes behind Marinelli. Coppi spoke of retiring from the Tour. Jacques Goddet, the director of the event came to see him. What did he say? The boss of the Tour would reveal nothing. On the other hand, the next morning in an editorial, it was discovered that he was disappointed. You could read it all under the heading, 'Signor Fausto Coppi is not a man of the Tour.'

' ....It was appalling to see this superior class rider, this intelligent and reflective man who had so much wanted the Tour, drifting helplessly, reclaiming the right to retire like a sick child demanding his medicine, without replying to his team mates who were encouraging him, cooling him down, feeding him. Whatever the reasons for such helplessness - and they do exist - it is not the fact that a man of the Tour does not know how to resist the bites of the famous witch with the green teeth, to renounce at the first hard blow and not know how to limit the damage. I am afraid that the feudal regime to which Signor Fausto Coppi has become accustomed is the real cause of the problem. Like all human beings, athletes who have had things too easy and have known to much success... have little resistance to pain...'

While Jacques Goddet was drawing up his article, Coppi still had not gone back on his decision to retire. In the evening, the 'Campionissimo' did not share the dinner table with the others. He ate alone in his room and, after the meal, his faithful 'gregari' Pezzi, Ricci and Milano went up to see him.

'What's happened ? asked Lucciano Pezzi. You are not going to retire without a real reason? The Tour is yours for the taking. There's still the Pyrenees and the Alps...'

And Pezzi too insisted. Suddenly Fausto decided to unload what he had in his heart.

'When I fell, my machine was broken. I asked for another bike. Binda was not there and the breakdown vehicle gave me a bike that was not my size.

'That's not the reason why you're going to retire'

'It's not about the bike. You understand that when I saw that Binda was not there my moral took a dive. Binda didn't want to help me, he's here for Bartali. He doesn't want me to win the Tour. When I started at the front it was his job to stay behind me, not with Bartali who was a long way behind.'

That was the truth. At the time no members of the press knew this. The mystery of the St Malo stage was quite simply 'the Binda affair'. In a shattered Fausto, a spring was broken and the machine did not want to start. The words of his Bianchi team manager Giovanni Tragella helps to make the situation a little clearer.

'Fausto is not a weak man but a sensitive one. For nothing his mood changes. Even his confidence and strength declines.

However, that evening the 'gregari' had not beaten their heads against the wall for nothing. In a low voice Coppi agreed to start the next day. He seemed to have changed his feelings towards Binda by the time he came to see him in his room. And it was a serene and theatrical team manager, who, a little later emphasised to the journalists;

'We spoke calmly. I do not take away the right of a rider to retire if he does not feel that he can continue, but frankly this does not seem to be the case here. Tomorrow is a long stage but an easy one and then there is a rest day. Following that there is a time trial that Fausto can win in an armchair.....'

Which is exactly what happened over the 92 kilometres between Sables d'Orlonne and La Rochelle.

This time Jacques Goddet was obliged to radically change his adjectives from those he used at St Malo:

'It is impossible to dislike the progress of Coppi as the kilometres slip beneath his wheels. His pedalling style is as pure as the Divine Comedie...unique!'

The first verbal skirmish between Bartali and Coppi occurred just before the Pyrenees. At the end of the stage, at San Sebastian, Coppi accused Bartali of having attacked and of having wanted to slip into a break. Binda intervened immediately.

' Bartali went but only because the danger was Robic. I was there and saw everything.'

Things calmed down again. The mountains came into sight in the distance. The first act of the Tour was over. A tragedy was avoided. St Malo was forgotten.

Going from San Sebastian to Pau, Magni announced that he wanted 'to do the stage'. It was certainly his right to do so as he was part of the 'cadetti' team who had no links with the Italian national team. His plan was successful. He stole the yellow jersey from Marinelli.

The next day was a rest day. Binda took advantage of it to hold a council of war:

'Tomorrow Coppi will play his card in the mountains. Ideally Bartali should escape with him as well. This will be quite a hard blow for the others. Tragellia and I will be behind them in two cars. Tragellia will have Fausto's spare bike and I will have Gino's. As I've already said the Tour will not be decided in the Pyrenees but it will give us a leg up for the two Alpine stages.'

Were the ' two greats' in agreement? On the scales Bartali registered 67 kilos, his ideal weight: Coppi was 74 kilos to prove that he too was on form.

'The inimitable masseur Pelizza told the Italian journalists:

'Fausto will win the Tour with one leg. I know it because each day that goes by he is in a worse temper. When he is like that, it is a sign that sooner or later he is going to explode and nobody will be able to resist him. He will pass over them like a steamroller on the flat and in the mountains.'

On the stage Pau to Luchon, Coppi proved himself to be the best but, being the victim of several punctures, he had to leave the stage victory to Jean Robic. The big exploit had not materialised but Binda's prediction was right: the Pyrenees did not decide the race.

Coppi riding one of the time-trial stages in the 1948 Tour de France

A First Double

The first great battle of the Tour de France of 1949 was expected between Cannes and Briancon on Monday 18th July.

The alarm clock rang at 4.00am and Coppi was one of the last to come downstairs. He was lazing around in his room. Bartali went to the mass which had been specially arranged for him.

From the start Kubler played the spoilsport. He was rejoined at the bottom of the Col de L'Izoard where Coppi and Bartali entered onto the scene. Even before the climb on the false flat of the Arvieux, the two Italian champions were relaying each other perfectly and in twenty kilometres they were to put 3'30" into Robic and more than 4 minutes into the other favourites.

An entente cordial, almost a fraternal one had begun between the two men. It was scarcely believable. Suddenly Fausto's back wheel found a pothole in the mud and the rider slid onto his side. Gino waited for him and gave him a hand up.

Without really wanting to Coppi accelerated and Bartali was hard put to follow him. But the man from Piedmont knew that his team mate as well as his rival was nevertheless celebrating his thirty fifth birthday on this very day. He was to be the first to wish him well. They entered the 'Casse Deserte', a decor of the same dimensions of the Tour. No one was interested in what was happening behind, only the two Italians counted. Coppi crossed over the summit in the lead with Bartali at his side. The latter punctured but Coppi waited for him.

The breathtaking descent to Briancon was completed. For the Tuscan's birthday, Coppi decided to let him take victory and the race lead. There still remained the second battle of the Alps between Briancon and St Vincent d'Aosta by the Cols of Montgenevre, Mont-Cenis, Iseran, and the Little St Bernard. The first part of the stage developed into a struggle between Robic and Bartali. Then on the last few bends before the summit of the Col de L'Iseran, Coppi came out of his reserve. In just one hundred metres the damage was considerable; he left Ockers and Apo Lazarides, devoured Bartali and left Robic continuing on his

Coppi and Bartali. They finished the Tour de France in this order

way alone to the summit. On the descent he was to be joined by a small group including Bartali. On the climb up the Little St Bernard, both Coppi and Bartali went onto the offensive. The two champions entered onto Italian soil to be acclaimed with passionate cries. At the bottom of the descent, there was a dramatic incident. Bartali raised his arm. He had just been the victim of a puncture. Coppi waited for him, freewheeling. He changed his wheel and got back in the saddle but on a bend was betrayed by the slippery road and fell. He was suffering from a twisted ankle and his shoulder was hurting. One minute went past and then two.

Coppi then asked a motorcyclist, Reschini, working for the Italian radio, what he should do and requested him to get the answer from Binda.

'Tell him to ride for his own account,' was the reply from the Italian manager.

There remained 42 kilometres to St Vincent d'Aosta and Coppi swallowed them with ease to take the yellow jersey. The level of Fausto's performance is best summed up by looking at the figures. The mountain stages, that is to say from the root of the Col d'Aubisque, in the Pyrenees to the 'summit' at Aosta, in the Alps, he taken back 55 minutes from Jacques Marinelli, who was leading the general classification. What mastery! How was it possible to better exploit the mountain roads, the climbs, the descents and the valleys. By winning this Tour de France he pulled off another masterstroke: winning the two major Tours in the same year, Italy and France, for the first time in history. Andre Ledcuq, twice winner of the Tour de France, who, this time had followed the 'Grand Boucle' in the guise of a journalist, breathlessly wrote the following:

'There are no more climbs at 14 or 18%, no more abrupt cols; no more calvary..... All is easy... The journalists, the riders, must have exaggerated. The mountains ? What a joke!....Seeing that under our eyes there is a man, just like the others, with his hands well placed on the handlebars which he is touching rather than holding, seeing that he is nailed to the saddle, that his long legs fall with composure on the pedals, the fine limbs with the lightness of a gazelle; seeing that the ankles at the bottom of the stroke make a graceful rounded movement which is so fascinating that you would want to see it in slow motion at the cinema.

No swaying of the hips or of the shoulders, everything turns as if in oil...

So what mysterious force makes this harmonious combination of athlete and machine advance? Then there is the rest, just as interesting to dissect. The long face like the blade of a knife, those inquisitive eyes, that mouth hardly open and calmly breathing the air. Not a grimace, never a complaint. Not a smile either but a constant application. Coppi studies the road ahead of him, looking for the summit, scrutinising the ground just in front of his wheel in order to avoid a flat tyre. He climbs like artists paint water-colours, without any apparent extra effort. How can this be? It is a mystery. Because when all is said and done Coppi only has two legs, two lungs, one heart, like you and I, and like all other contestants of the Tour...'

If he did not become world champion on the road, he did on the other hand take the title on the track in pursuit, beating Gillen of Luxembourg in the final. Then he became Champion of Italy before chalking up a fourth victory in the Tour of Lombardy.

The series of successes became dazzling; not enough however to satisfy Giulia Locatelli who could no longer stay still in the middle of the crowd. When she saw him arrive almost always victorious she immediately rushed forward, knowing however in advance that she would come up against the smiles and the mockeries of other fans which her audacious élan provoked. She did reach him, he held out his hand. When the wall of people pushed her back again, she went regularly to see the police who were guarding the changing rooms at the velodrome, for example. Then she played her 'number', lying outrageously and making herself pass for a personality, distributing handshakes to people that she had never seen or conversely treating them in an insolent manner until someone finally let her enter.

After several months she came to the conclusion that the way to the changing rooms was less congested and less guarded than the finish line, so she could approach Fausto without having her clothes disarrayed by the mob, without having her hair ruffled. And above all she could speak to him.

Soon Fausto was no longer hard put to recognise her. He remembered that she was 'there last time' and her permanent way of following all the Italian races.

It was he who later warned the guardians of the changing rooms that if a lady in white arrived - one with blue eyes - tall and elegant, they must let her through.

Later still Fausto would know all about her and her family.

Finally, it would be he who would become impatient if by chance she arrived late, or did not arrive at all.

When she could not get there, she listened to the sporting exploits of her favourite rider on the radio. She was not in love with Coppi. He was only 'her' champion. She would put up with anything to see him win, to see his name printed in large type on the front page of the newspapers.

'For me', she would say, 'he is not only a marvellous human machine, two wheels which race in a breathtaking manner, a machine of muscles, an élan of strength and of youth which leaves me breathless.'

The man Fausto Coppi did not exist in her eyes. The champion who was so much admired could not be a man. It was a being who caused an immense joy or a terrible pain. Nobody could envisage a normal connection with him. You could be for him, with him, but whether you knew him or not you could not be involved with him.

Mrs Locatelli 'followed' Fausto Coppi blindly. Whenever she saw him, she pushed herself to the front and shouted 'Fausto, Fausto, you are a God!'

At Vareno the rumour spread as fast as a trail of gunpowder: the doctor's wife had become mad over cycling, she was also a fan of Fausto Coppi more unrelenting than the most ardent 'tifosi'. That was saying something!

This new passion fed the conversations in the homes. The husbands announced it to their wives, the wives told it to their children and the children ran after Giulia in the street.

Just a few steps away from her home, in the butchers of the grocers, she found on entering the shop graffiti deprecating Coppi: the double V followed by the name 'Bartali', 'Long Live Bartali!', 'Down With Coppi!'

Fausto & Serse Coppi at the grave of Marcel Cerdan,
while in North Africa in 1949

THE DIVERTED TRAJECTORY

AT THE END OF THE MONTH OF MAY 1950, Dr Locatelli and his wife decided to take a few days holiday. At the time, the Tour of Italy had just started. Part of their plans was to go to vantage points on one of the mountains in the Dolomites.

The previous year Coppi had dropped everyone on these very same climbs, and Giulia thought it reasonable to believe that he would be doing the same in 1950.

In this Tour of Italy, a young man started of whom people were saying very nice things. He was Swiss and had been discovered by the ex-World Champion, Learco Guerra, he was called Hugo Koblet.

On the 9th stage Vincenza-Bolzano, Fausto decided to attack as a way of testing his form. but before he was able to put his plan into action, a drama intervened.

At the sixtieth kilometre while the riders were on the descent of the Pemolano, a modest rider, Amando Peverelli, made an involuntary mistake; Coppi became unbalanced. His back wheel touched Amando's front wheel. It is only fair to mention the fact the latter was suffering from a slight disability as he had lost the sight in one eye following an accident in the Alps in the 1949 Tour de France. In the course of the Tour of Italy in 1950 Peverelli had not seen Coppi who had just overtaken him on his blind side.

Guiseppi Ambrosini, a director of the Gazetto dello Sport was a witness:

'It was a bad crash which sent Fausto to the ground, moulded in his sky blue jersey to which the number one was pinned. A cold shiver went through my veins. Like a madman I jumped out of the car and grabbed him under the armpits to lift him up. He was groaning with a voice that was hardly audible. When I hoisted him onto my shoulders and his right leg touched the ground he let out a scream of pain. His shorts were torn at the right hip. There was no blood which led me to hope that the injury was not too serious. his face became very pale and he seemed to have no strength. Tears started to come from his eyes. We sponged his head down and straightaway tried to put him back on his bike but the mere action of lifting his right leg gave him unbearable pain.

'I can't, I can't' he groaned 'I must have broken something!'

Dr Camillo Campi ran up, gave him an injection, then the other race followers tried in their turn to put him back in the saddle. This time after the first movement he was immobilised with the pain. Then the ambulance arrived and took him to the hospital of Santa Chiara at Trento, some fifty kilometres away.

During this time, on the slopes of one of the mountains of the Dolomites, the official radio car of the race was passing between two banks of spectators. Through the loudspeaker Giulia heard Coppi's name, she pricked up her ears but at first she could not make out what the announcer was saying.

After a few seconds, the announcement was repeated on the next bend and she heard:

'Coppi has fallen on the descent of Premolano. He has been transported to hospital at Trento!'

With an anxious face she turned towards her husband:

'I want to go and see him, I want to see him!'...

'But you're mad! They won't let any 'foreigners' into a hospital. perhaps they'll be obliged to operate. It all depends on the seriousness of the injury. They'll never let us see him. Even I would be thrown out of the door. And you can imagine what the journalists will be like.'

She remained incorrigible and caused a real scene, stamping her feet and saying the same thing over and over again.

After a few minutes the doctor relented in the face of such a barrage, she just refused to take no for an answer.

With great difficulty they managed to extricate their car from the numerous vehicles which were crowded into the area. The road to Trento opened before them.

In room 20 at the hospital Coppi, in great pain, learned that his rival Bartali had beaten the two Swiss, Hugo Koblet and Ferdi Kubler, in the sprint to win the stage.

Bartali brought his winner's bouquet to his adversary.

He was there, broken by misfortune, on his bed of suffering when the Locatelli couple presented themselves at the gates of the establishment. Giulia took the initiative of going to speak to the gatekeeper who immediately called the duty doctor.

'Doctor, this lady wants to see Coppi!'

It was a young doctor who was plunged into embarrassment and seemed exhausted by his spell on duty. He shook his head:

'Madam, please do not insist. I tell you that it is not possible. Professor Pazzi who is our head, has given very strict orders. The patient needs a lot of care. We must not tire him out.'

At that moment a noise made her jump. Giulia saw a woman who was accompanied by a blind man. It was Bruna, Coppi's wife, who had Biagio Cavanna on her arm.

So she could see for sure that the injured man was receiving visitors. This made her all the more determined.

While the young doctor was still close to her, she took him to one side and begged him:

'Please, telephone Coppi and explain to him that we have come here specially to see him.'

'What name shall I give him?'

'Dr Locatelli and his wife.'

The young doctor probably thinking that a phone call would liberate him from this forceful lady, dialled the number of Fausto's room.

The reply was immediate:

'They are my friends, I will willingly see them.'

The Campionissimo was stretched out on a bed with a cage to keep the blankets off his leg. His face was very pale and his forehead and cheeks were covered in sweat. When he tried to smile his face tightened into a grimace of pain.

He tried to lift himself up but fell back immediately. None of the three broke the silence; Fausto was the first to speak:

'It was rotten luck...It's strange...Just today when I was feeling so good.'

The silence returned. Fausto tried once again to smile and addressed himself to Giulia's husband:

'You can see, doctor, the inconvenience of the profession of a cyclist. This is how I find myself at present...Thank you Mrs. Giulia, thank you doctor. They say that I'll never be able to race again. Would you like to look doctor?'

Coppi uncovered himself and showed the plaster the area of the fracture.

Coming out of the hospital, Locatelli said to his wife:

'It's a serious affair but he has the means to recover. The hospital is quite well equipped. The chief orthopaedist - the man who is treating him - is one of the best in Italy. He will get better.'

However, the verdict was serious: triple fracture of the pelvis.

The champion was quite bitter over the accident as he was looking forward to the 1950 season to confound the peninsula's press who often picked on him as a target. At the beginning of the season they had written:

'Coppi will win no races in 1950 because he will pay for the efforts that he produced last year.'

In actual fact he had not won the Milan San-Remo. But what impression had he given? Victim of a puncture in the crucial part of the race, he quickly rejoined the men in front with a stupefying ease, his mouth wide open, his eyes sticking out of his head. He was capable of the phenomenal effort of climbing the Capo Berta, one of the principal difficulties of the race, at forty kilometres and hour. Bartali, who had previously taken advantage of Coppi's puncture, had attacked to put some distance between them. He threw him a malevolent glance when he saw him come back so quickly and vexed, he refused to collaborate in the success of the break. The result was that the field reformed and the Tuscan won the bunch sprint.

Coppi left the race depressed. Certain papers continued their relentless attack on him as the Milan daily wrote:

'Fausto Coppi is not at home in Italian events or races such as the Tour de France, and his style is not suited to the character of the great international classics.'

Cut to the quick by this, he paid a visit to his team manager Tragella to draw up a plan of battle for the most prestigious of all road races: Paris -Roubaix. Pinalla di Grandi, his mechanic, built up a machine specially adapted to the cobblestones of the North. He would be surrounded by solid and faithful men, his 'gregari' Conte, Pasquini, Crippa, Milano, Carrea and Serse Coppi.

A great day was being prepared for, something to make him forget all his misfortunes.

He chose the feeding station at Arras to attack. Some time before the two courageous men, Gino Sciardis and Maurice Diot were away on their own. The champion of Italy suddenly joined them. Sciardis was soon dropped and then it was Diot's turn to let him go. This veritable rocket produced the demonstration of a lifetime. There were forty five kilometres to the finish, forty five kilometres that Coppi devoured in a style and in a purity rarely to be equalled, continuing to increase his advantage. During the last hour of the race he struggled alone on the pavements which were hardly rideable and on the terrible roads he covered more than forty one kilometres in one hour.

Some time later, he did it again in the Flèche Wallonne, another international classic by again winning alone, this time the demonstration lasted for one hundred kilometres.

What could the Italian press write this time?

He wanted to win the Tour of Italy and the Tour de France by a knockout. Only - it was stated - could bad luck prevent him.

Fausto was consumed with sadness in his hospital at Trento. He had seen Giulia, his number one supporter, go away. He was surprised to be thinking about her. The wife of the doctor, she too was thinking about him, perhaps in a more intimate way. Did she consider him still as a champion or did she perceive him more as a man?

Difficult to say at this stage. Giulia herself did not even know. What

Paris-Roubaix 1950. Coppi established a new record. On his wheel, Maurice Diot,who would soon be dropped

she did know was that she would apply herself to get to know him more by writing to him. And so her admiration for him became even greater. She knew, for example that during his cycling career, the man from Piedmont knew only a single rule in his life: to train, to eat, to sleep and to race. Never was he diverted from this programme.

In everyday life he was nothing like the image people had of the malleable athlete. Once Bartali called him the 'skinned cat' and it was quite a faithful image. His unattractive outline was not helped by the narrow shoulders, his chicken-like calves, his unusually long legs, a short chest and a unimpressive torso. One would willingly venture to say that the bones were protruding through the skin so much that they appeared to be heavy. They were in fact brittle and would break like glass. His skeleton was poorly developed, no doubt due to malnutrition as a child. During his infancy he must have suffered from rickets.

He was only himself on a bike. His long limbs became incomparable harmonious lines. And he had in his pedalling movement, a sort of lightness, of fluidity, of celestial essence. No champion at this level gave such an impression of fragility, of vulnerability. From all this came, no doubt, his strange magnetism. After such a close inspection of his body it is astonishing to know that he eventually got on a bicycle and became a super-champion.

'Fausto is admirably well balanced, Dr Campi recognised, but in the sense of his length. His internal secretions and his hormones give him his power more than his muscles which are not powerful but well balanced. He is a perfect example of the great champions with long muscles.'

The 'Campionissimo' frankly did not really look like an athlete. On the other hand he could be classed among the athletes of cycling as his long carcass became strangely balanced and supple when he pedalled.

If you speak of him as having light and fragile bodywork, the specialists quickly add that he has an unusually powerful engine, an ideal power to weight ratio. With regard to this only enormous thigh muscles are in any way astonishing. It is generally said that: 'He was born to pedal. He does not know what it is to have dead weight and useless muscles.'

In a race all of the muscles used in the effort of cycling were developed to the point of abnormality while the others left the impression of weakness.

On his bike, his long thin legs turned like connecting rods in a well maintained machine. No hiccup ever troubled this marvellous mechanism with a strange silhouette and a perfect aerodynamism. The chest crouched over more but stayed well in line, the head was pushed into the shoulders, and the mouth opened lightly and breathing through the nose was abandoned in the intensity of the effort. He was compared to a Heron.

Dr Campi added other details:

'He has a heart which beats very slowly, a thoracic cage almost deformed with a suppleness of rubber and a capacity of seven litres with a normal intake of breath, an exceptional suprarenal gland which has a beneficial effect on the blood and tenacious will-power.'

For the moment we are in June 1950 and for Coppi it was the beginning of long days of immobility. Through the open window he could see the countryside dominated by the Dolomites which had led both to his fame and to his misfortune.

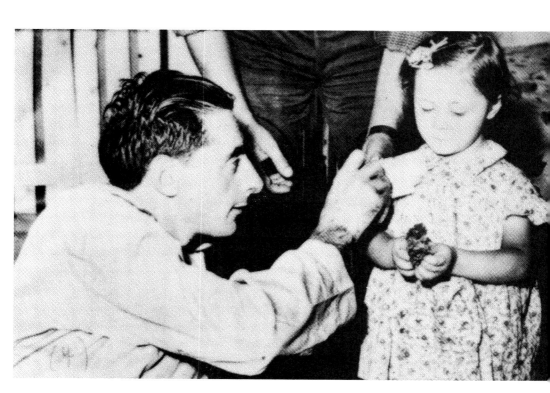

THE TRAGEDY

AFTER TWENTY NINE DAYS OF IMMOBILITY, Coppi left the Santa Chiara hospital and was taken to the village of Rocegno, to the Hotel des Thermes situated a little way up the valley of the Adige; a desirable move as the climate at Trento in the summer proved to be unbearable.

The wife of Dr Locatelli did not come back to see him but that did not stop her writing to him. Fausto replied and a correspondence blossomed. She addressed her letters to Giovanni Chiesa, the friend who passed them on and Coppi addressed his to the post office at Varese.

'We observed a sort of strictness in our messages, she emphasised; we told each other nothing intimate. Each day I received a letter; each day I sent one. These two events from then on made my life more fulfilled at Varano Borghi'.

At the start of the 1951 season the correspondence continued, if a little more spaced out due to the demands of the racing calendar. Coppi threw himself into training with the enthusiasm of a debutante. On the Riviera he no longer felt the effects of his crash in the Tour of Italy. All his muscles responded. No more gnawing pain in the thighs; the legs refound their suppleness and his kidneys were working marvellously.

He said he was ready for Milan-San Remo. Before hand the smaller classic Milan-Turin would serve as final preparation.

It was 11th March. The rain did not stop falling and the cold wind started to blow. After several skirmishes, Coppi decided on the climb of La Serra to make the move to decide the race. It was a dazzling attack. Only a few men were able to follow him. There were five of them in the lead under the beating rain. Would the organisers stick to the plan of finishing the race on the Turin track or would they move the arrival point to the road alongside it? But finally no change was made and the riders entered the track in the following order: Martini was first with Coppi on his wheel, then followed Magni, Soldani and Albani. They had to ride a complete lap of the track and then it was the finish. Suddenly Magni attacked, Coppi seemed to be surprised but made his effort out of the saddle two hundred and fifty metres from the finishing

line. The surface was slippery and his tyres couldn't grip the cement. He fell. The Campionissimo had hurt his left shoulder and was crying in pain. The diagnosis revealed a fractured clavicle. An operation was necessary and Professor Dogliatti, one of the best Italian surgeons was going to perform it.

Fausto simply wanted a local anaesthetic so that he could closely follow the meticulous work of the doctors. The operation was successful. The shoulder did not need to be plastered; his left arm was in a silk sling attached round his neck.

He hoped to ride a good Tour of Italy. Unfortunately he committed the error of restarting training too quickly and in the Giro he found himself for the first time in his career incapable of reacting to all of the attacks of his rivals. This in no way prevented him from winning the time trial and from taking a stage in the Dolomites at Bolzano after having taken second place the day before behind Louison Bobet with whom he had escaped. He finally finished fourth in the Tour of Italy, which was not so bad considering that it was just a few weeks away from the start of the Tour de France.

His rendez-vous before the Tour de France was the Tour of Piedmont on the 29th June. He had no idea of the drama that was waiting. During the course of the event, Coppi did not show himself at the front. Wisely installed in the middle of the bunch, he was preparing for the final sprint in the company of his brother Serse. On the Corso Casale at Turin, a few hundred metres from the velodrome, there was a crash. Fausto turned his head and saw his brother tangled up on the ground with his machine. He had crashed heavily and hit the edge of the pavement. Helped by several other riders, he got up straight away. The big brother continued and as soon as he crossed the finishing line he was anxious to know what had happened to Serse. Coppi hurried to see his brother. Serse was complaining of head pains and these pains got worse and worse. He groaned and called for his mother and Fausto. It was decided to transport him immediately to the Sanatrix clinic where Fausto himself had been hospitalised after his crash in the Milan-Turin race. Two hours only had passed since the accident. Professor Dogliatti examined him. Serse had already lost consciousness. The professor turned to Fausto and said that his mother must be informed. Coppi then understood that there was no hope. In fact even before they tried to operate, Serse died.

The champion, very badly shaken and filled with grief by this tragedy still could not believe what had happened. Serse was his faithful and attentive shadow, his best friend and most devoted team mate. He remembered the jerky pedalling style, which was the consequence of the shortening of a leg following a serious accident. He remembered the turbulent child always ready to joke. At school he was the despair of the teachers. When he returned to Castellania after having

At the farm in Castellania, Coppi with his mother, remembering the happier times with brother Serse

participated in several races, village children came out to meet him. They accompanied him to the doorstep of his house and asked to play with them. Serse never refused. Although tired by the journey, he was always able to find ten minutes and a little goodwill to satisfy them.

After which, Coppi's state of mind understandably took a turn for the worse. The day following this horrible accident, the Campionissimo announced to the press:

'I am giving up the Tour de France and will probably give up cycling altogether.'

Fausto would always remember Serse on this accursed day. He remembered that, the night before he started out for the fatal Tour of Piedmont he had a premonition. He had slept at Castellania and he woke up, nervous and worried saying to his aunt Albina:

'During the night a dog would not stop howling. It gave me a strange feeling, as if it was going to bring me bad luck.'

Then he took his small case containing his racing clothing and went down to the kitchen. After breakfast he got up to leave but still seemed very worried. He touched every object on the table. There was a statuette on the mantelpiece which he kept picking up and putting down. He went to the door and came back again shaking his head. He went away without saying anything, got into the car with the bicycle in the back. He embraced his 'mamma' who told him, as always to be careful. Serse drove very quickly and Angiolina trembled when she knew he was at the wheel.

'My brother,' Fausto said, 'loved Castellania, the people there and the houses on the hill of San Alloggio, its earth was fertile but hard to cultivate. He loved it all with the naive soul of a big child. He dreamed of being able, one day after having given up the profession of racing cyclist, of having a nice little house built with a piece of land and a cowshed with some cattle. Not regaining consciousness, God had treated him generously for he would have suffered too much that morning if he knew that he was saying good-bye to his 'little house on the hill.'

Fortunately for the sporting world, the idol of Italy changed his mind about the Tour de France. If the disappearance of his beloved brother left him destroyed, he knew that the public was waiting for him. He fulfilled their expectations by saying; 'It's my duty to race.' However, the main question was: 'Is he really at the level of being able to put up with the vicissitudes of this 38th Tour de France ?'

This Tour was raced at a very fast pace and one man in particular was impressing everyone: the Swiss Hugo Koblet. Coppi knew already by this time that victory would go to this Adonis that the singer Jacques Grello had baptised the 'pedaller of charm'. He was inferior in all departments to this man from Zurich who was in a 'state of grace'. Would Coppi have been so dominated by him if he had not been so diminished by the misfortune that had struck him? Nobody will ever know.

He had the most terrible day on the sixteenth stage from Carcassonne to Montpellier in a suffering heat. He was dropped like the most mediocre rider and found himself far behind, in the company with his 'gregari' who had waited for him. Magnificent in defeat, he fought to the very end. It was a poignant tableau. Haggard, vomiting, zigzagging, one sometimes had the impression that he was going to collapse onto the burning tarmac. Lacking in strength and willpower, having nothing more to hope for than commiseration, he was afraid of being pitied, Coppi never spoke of retiring. There is in this gesture, which appeared so useless as the poor champion seemed no longer in a state where he could turn the pedals, evidence of the astonishing respect for the moral contract of the Tour de France rider which is linked to heroism. When he crossed the finishing line at Montpellier, more than thirty minutes had ticked past since Koblet had won the stage.

The next day, the rest day was welcomed by everyone tired after sixteen days of intense effort.

At the Hotel Metrople at Montpellier, Fausto received a visit from his unhappy wife Bruna. She wanted him to give up cycling at all costs, emphasising that she would never be the same after Serse's death. For Fausto she feared the worst. While her husband was looking for moral support she was doing the opposite and this was beginning to irritate him. He would have preferred to have known that she was at home. Why had she come? Cycling was her husband's life, it was what he enjoyed doing. He had to honour his contracts for the sake of the public. 'I have sworn to finish this Tour that I started and I will be at the finish at the Parc des Princes' he wrote to Giulia. At least the doctor's wife understood the situation.

Madame Coppi had grasped nothing, thought Fausto. She has not just gone through this terrible nightmare on the road which I have just experienced. She has not seen her husband pallid and coughing on his bike and being splattered from head to toe, she has not seen him on the point of collapsing into a ditch; she has not seen him dragging his big body under the fiery sun of the Black Mountain, groaning as he climbed the Col de la Baraque-de-Bral and then hesitating before plunging down the long descent to Lodeve.

Coppi loved his profession. The distress grew. Madame Coppi did not understand anymore; even when a recovered Fausto several days later carried off one of the finest stages of the Tour from Gap to Briancon by way of the Cols of the Vars and the Izoard. Certainly he could no longer win the 'Grand Boucle' - that was for Hugo Koblet to do - but he nevertheless made a big comeback.

Serse Coppi on his death bed in 1951. Fausto, devastated with pain, talks of giving up cycling

Coppi and his wife Bruna

Coppi avoiding the cobbles of Paris-Roubaix 1952

Towards a New Double

After the Tour de France 1951, Coppi gave best to Koblet again in the Grand Prix des Nations at Paris. Bad luck would not leave him. A high fever had already stopped him competing in the World Championships... On the 14th October he was at the start of the Grand Prix of Lugano, a time trial that was promoted as a revenge 'match' after the Grand Prix des Nations. In fact very few journalists saw it that way. Fausto showed them that they were wrong. The Italian refound the form of his greater days. He led the race from start to finish and Koblet was submitted to the humiliation of being caught by his rival.

In the Tour of Lombardy, after having tried several attempts at escaping, he finally figured in the decisive break but was out sprinted by Louison Bobet and Minardi.

The season came to an end and he wanted to conserve his good physical form so as to be ready for the start of the 1952 season. He rode the Paris Six-Day with Teruzzi and finished fourth.

In this new season, success was not quick to come. In Milan-San Remo, he was beaten by one of his team mates, a young man with great promise: Loretto Petrucci. In Paris-Roubaix he deserved victory a hundred times over but had to submit to the sprint of the Belgian Rik Van Steenbergen. The writer Serge Groussard who followed the race for 'Miroir des Sports' wrote in his report:

'Coppi was leading the decisive break. jumping from he cobblestones to the pavement in a cloud of dust, shaving the noses of an inconceivable crowd which was screaming his name more than any of the others....He had a distant expression on his face. One would have said that he was going for a stroll! Like all the others he was blackened, completely covered in mud, but his pedalling was relaxed, his expression was calm behind his dark glasses. His body was scarcely moving, rather like a branch in the wind, and this movement seemed to have nothing to do with effort.....I remember the photos you used to see of the former champions pushing desperately on their pedals with a mask of grimaces and wrinkles, their bodies bent as if being tortured. And here was this man repudiating all this with his speed and fury, denying it with his impassive expression, his obsession to win....It was real style. It was the man alone and through it all he maintained an attitude which demonstrated a sort of impartial indifference....'

In the Tour of Italy, he began by winning the time trial stage and could wait confidently for the Alps to 'impose his law' in company with a team-mate of his own choice, Raphel Geminiani. The Frenchman put on the sidelines by the French teams was picked up by Bianchi at Coppi's express wish. From the beginning of the Giro, the two men were agreed on the tactics to adopt:

'There are too many riders who stay on my wheel and want me to lose, the champion revealed. You will attack every day.....if you can. The others will be obliged to race after you, so the roles will be reversed and I will attack them when I judge it to be necessary.'

The plan was followed to the letter in the mountains and the adversaries fell into the trap. Coppi dominated this Tour of Italy with insolent ease, massacring his rivals. Once again Bartali had to bow his head. The rivalry was always there, often going beyond the strict bounds of sportsmanship. A strong incompatibility of mood continued to be demonstrated.

'Fausto, Geminiani recounted, felt himself to be superior to the Tuscan who he reproached for systematically exploiting his work, and that of his team mates.' This manner of holding back did nothing to damage his popularity. In this Gino Bartali was the Champion of Italy and as such was displaying his red, white and green jersey. The spectators easily recognised him and acclaimed him. This irritated Fausto a great deal, already annoyed by the frequent goings and comings of Gino to the Vatican. An idea came to him to confound his hypocritical rival. In the Bianchi team was Donato Piazza, an enormous man, who was a Champion of Italy on the track. One evening Fausto collared him: 'From now on you will wear your national jersey'- But the rules only allow me to wear it on the track, Piazza replied.

'No matter! Do what I say'. And the colossus complied. Riding at the front of the bunch, the bunch greeted him with cries of 'viva Bartali' and 'Dai Gino' so enthusiastically that nobody noticed the real Bartali go past.

As a consequence of the operation Coppi paid the daily fines inflicted on Donato Piazza, guilty of having infringed the rules. By the finish it had cost him a lot of money. But he was happy as his trap had worked remarkably well.

On the other hand Coppi - winner of the Tour of Italy- was not at the end of his problems. He refused to take part in the Tour de France if Bartali was present. On the 10th June at Milan a preliminary meeting for the Tour de France took place and brought them face to face at the table of the Association of Italian Cycle Manufacturers. As Bartali entered Coppi declared:

'I do not want to see a repetition of the situation which existed in the 49 and 51 Tours. In actual fact I found myself alone for the greater part of the race to control our rivals, to chase after them, and bring them to reason, while you gently followed in the wake of the team and stayed in my shadow waiting for me to wear myself out....'

'It's true Fausto, our styles of racing are different. But I am coming to help you. I have no bellicose intentions. I do not want to make life hard for you. I promise to collaborate and I will.'

Bartali wanted to be conciliatory but Coppi did not change his position and launched himself once again onto the attack.

'There is only one thing which interests you: to get to Paris in front of me. You are not interested in anything else. You will be quite happy to be 80th if I am 81st.'

The discussion reached an impasse. It needed several days and all the diplomacy of Alfredo Binda to finally, one evening at Bordighera, get the antagonists to agree. Everything was settled, the curtain could therefore be raised on the Tour de France at Brest.

Where was Coppi going to enter the scene? That depended on the race of course. Everyone had to wait for the fifth stage to see him really in action. The Tour went into Belgium and the Luxemburger Jean Diederich had already escaped. He was hardly any worry to Fausto who in turn got out of the saddle. The attack was launched, Coppi was alone. The beautiful machine started to function. The speedometers on the following cars went up to 45-48 kph. It was a royal escape. He finished second on the stage. Bartali crossed the line two minutes later. The confirmation of his remarkable physical form came during the seventh stage from Metz to Nancy.

With a perfect aerodynamic style, he 'swallowed' the miles. Alfedo Binda standing up in his car was observing him closely. A first incident materialised at the beginning of the race. Victim of a puncture, he saw his mechanic Umberto Marnati rush towards him but in his haste, instead of arriving with a front wheel he had brought a back one as the seconds ticked past. Beside himself, Coppi cried out:

'Give me a revolver to shoot this idiot!'

The Italian punctured again in the last twenty kilometres. This time Marnati passed him the 'right' wheel and Coppi won from the Belgian Roger Decock.

During these first few stages there was a 'waltz' of the yellow jersey. The Frenchman Nello Lauredi, a member of the French national team took the lead from the Italian Magni who regained it the next day at Mulhouse. The stage from Mulhouse to Lausanne saw one of the most bizarre moments of this Tour de France: Coppi's 'gregario', one of those

Bartali in front of Coppi and Lauredi, in the Vosges (Tour de France 1952)

Coppi decides it's the right time to go it alone (Tour de France 1952 10th Stage)

devoted to him body and soul, Andrea Carrea, became overall leader. The good and wise Sandrino - as Coppi called him - recognisable with his 'wicked fairy' face and his Cyranesque nose remained constantly at the front. He was always there on this stage, controlling the numerous attempts to escape. He grew increasingly worried as each time an offensive materialised no Italian joined in.....This looked as if it would put Magni's yellow jersey in jeopardy. So he slipped back to speak to Coppi.

'Fausto, he said, there is a non-stop battle going on. The Italians are never in it. If it continues like that a group is going to get away and it will be the right one, and so much for us. '

On that Coppi seemed to be somewhere else and rebuffed him.

'Do what you want!'

And Carrea as a faithful domestic watched over all the movements of the peloton....Suddenly with still a good way to go, a dozen men found themselves off the front. Notably there was the Frenchmen Marinelli and Remy, the Swiss Diggelman and the Dutchman Nolten......Carrea saw it all and joined them. He did not think the break would go very far. Anyway he was doing his duty. But his calculations were faulty. The gap grew and soon the finish was in sight. There was only one thing that Carrea wanted: that their advance was not so big that Magni would lose his yellow jersey. It was then that the situation turned into a comedy for the new yellow jersey was none other than the gregario Carrea.

He did not understand and cried when he put on the livery. He thought the sky had fallen in. How would Fausto take it? When the champion arrived a few minutes later, Carrea went towards him in tears to proffer his excuses.

You must understand that I did not want this jersey Fausto. I have no right to it. A poor man like me, the yellow jersey?

This episode relaxed the atmosphere in the Italian team and the Campionissimo always spoke of the event with a wry smile and said to the journalists at the end of the Tour:

'Ours is certainly a very hard profession with terrible demands and painful sacrifices. Carrea gave everything for me. In return I offered him only money. I know very well that if he was not my team mate he would earn much less, and when all is said and done he is happy and many of his comrades envy him, but I personally think he deserves more that what he has the right to: a little of the intoxication of the triumph. I had a way of settling part of my debt: it was to let him wear the jersey for a few days. Unfortunately, the next day, Robic started a big battle. I really had to bring him back and Andrea was dispossessed of his prize. Do you know what he said to the journalists the next evening after I had taken the jersey? That it was not right for a soldier to leave his

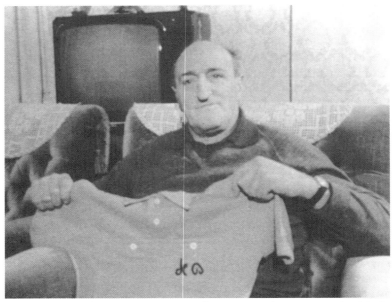

Andrea Carrea, gregario, yellow jersey in the 1952 Tour, fearful of incurring the wrath of his team leader, Coppi. The latter approved

Bottom : Coppi attacks, dropping Jean Robic (Sestrières-Alpe d'Huez, Tour de France 1952)

captain....'

It was by using the route towards the summit of Alpe d'Huez that first duel in the Alps took place.

The initial attack came from Jean Robic on one of the first bends. Raphael Geminiani jumped onto his wheel and then Fausto Coppi did. In the middle of the climb when Geminiani dropped back, the Italian tried a few small attacks but Robic was able to reply. But when the Campionissimo judged the time to be right to rid himself of the little Breton, he accelerated hard, threw him a couple of glances and went on alone to victory.

'On that day Coppi, wrote Felix Levitan in the 'Miroir du Tour', was not the normal Coppi, he was the unchained warrior, the big cat on the trial of his prey and because we were at his side on the motorbike, because we were scrutinising his face, because we could read it in his eyes, we would say that we saw there was an animal glint, cruel, such as a tiger would have leaping on his victim....'

He wore the yellow jersey of the Tour de France, his domestic Carrea now occupied second place on general classification.

The second act of the Alps was played out between Bourg d'Oisans and Sestrieres, which included the climbs of four cols and was similar to the previous one, which is to say that it was marked by the domination of the Italian champion.

He climbed the Croix-de-Fer in the lead but, estimating that the finish was still too far away, allowed himself to be rejoined on the descent. On the Col du Galibier, at ten kilometres from the summit, judging the moment to put his rivals in their place, he accelerated and immediately dropped Ruiz, Geminiani, Ockers and Bartali. Five kilometres from the top he rejoined the man who had escaped on the previous col - that of Telegraphe - a little Breton by way of the name of Jean Le Guilly and without giving him a glance went away alone to the top of the mountain and then launched himself onto the descent in order to enter Italian territory. His flight was extraordinary, unbelievable, magical.

An enormous clamour greeted his arrival at Sestrieres. It was necessary to wait a little more than seven minutes to see the arrival of the second man, Bernardo Ruiz and more than ten minutes for Gino Bartali.

The scene at the finish turned into delirium. The police cordons were broken, Fausto pulled here and there, owed his salvation to a group of carabiniers who had been kept in reserve.

So Coppi had inflicted a severe defeat on the rest of the field. Instead of exclaiming his joy, he excused himself, or almost, in front of the microphones which were held out to him:

'I was harassed on all the climbs: Lauredi, Lucien, Lazarides and Dotto on the Croix-de-Fer and Le Guilly on the Galibier. I finished up

In the Galiber, Coppi catches Le Guilly and then goes away alone (Tour de France 1952, 11th stage)

The first four in the 1952 Tour de France : Ruiz (3rd), Bartali (4th), Ockers (2nd) and Coppi (1st)

getting nervous, exhausted and, in my desire to give them a lesson I rode the stage in a very different way to what I planned. I wanted in fact to wait and see, to go away at the last possible moment on the climb to Sestrieres, exactly as I had done on the climb to Alpe d'Huez. I wanted to win in front of my compatriots, not to treat myself to a considerable lead.'

The Tour went down to Monaco. It was making its way towards the transition stages before Mont Ventoux. Sestrieres-Monaco was marked by an unexpected event. While the front group was riding hard up the Col de Castillon, Alfredo Binda, standing up in his car looked at Coppi and Bartali pedalling, the only two Italians in the little group. Suddenly he started to think very strange thoughts. ' If Coppi punctured, who would wait for him?' He had scarcely chased these bad dreams from his mind than there was Coppi, stopped with a flat tyre. The tube had exploded. What happened then? Bartali simply gave his wheel to Fausto. Binda wanted to kiss him......

On the Mont Ventoux stage, the same thing almost happened again. But this time Coppi told Bartali to carry on as he knew the faithful Carrea was just behind. Robic won the stage but the Tour was already decided save for a serious accident.

This engendered a lack of interest among the riders, the journalists and the spectators even to the point of boredom and melancholia. It was therefore no surprise when the organisers announced at Perpignan that the prizes allocated to the second and third placed men on general classification were to be raised respectively to five hundred thousand and two hundred and fifty thousand francs.

The Pyrenees confirmed, once again the incontestable superiority of the Italian champion. He won at Pau after leading over the top of the Aubisque and the Tourmalet. Coppi, King of the peloton could reign in the sunshine and in the rain.

He had no pity for the Dutchman, Jan Nolten. At the summit of the Puy de Dome, at 400 metres from the line, the giant 'Batave' still had a lead of one hundred metres but Coppi arrived to gobble up a rider who was one of the revelations of the Tour.

The Tour de France was won. Ockers finished second at more than twenty minutes. Bartali took fourth place, which was quite an achievement for an athlete of 38 years.

Andre Leducq, himself a double winner of the Tour de France, had the following to say:

'On all terrain's Coppi was at home....If it was a question of foiling an attack on the flat, he was able to do it, only letting breaks go that he wanted to. In this regard his clairvoyance was faultless and the least little group containing a man judged to be dangerous could not hope to get very far....If it was a question of climbing a mountain, there too he gave absolute proof of his superiority, dropping the best climbers of them all as he did at the Alpe d'Huez or Sestrieres, being content to keep them under surveillance and then leaving them so they only had the remaining crumbs to fight over. I ask myself if ever in the course of the history of the Tour de France a winner knew how to ally more strength to more wisdom, patience and intelligence.

In spite of a strong desire to find the smallest error or flaw in his armour, never was it possible for us to say or write: ' Today Fausto was mistaken'. His legs never betrayed him, neither did his nerves or his brains. He even knew how to resist - and this is by no means his smallest merit - the desire to crush his opponents on the flat like he could have done it he had really wanted to . He was happy with a single demonstration, but convincing one, on the Northern roads, when he went away at Namur, irresistible, just as he had been in Paris-Roubaix. On paper the plan was pleasing. However no tactics could have caused our man to stumble. Sometimes needled, he always came out of it with an accrued advantage. It was wrong to make him furnish an effort when he had decided to stay calm. The lamb was transformed into a lion...'

The Trials of Life

At the time of Coppi's finest triumphs, bad luck often played its part. On the 7th August while he was riding a track meeting at Perpigan, he crashed with his partner Berando Ruiz while making a change in a madison. They picked up Fausto with a broken shoulder blade and a crack in his left clavicle. The doctor prescribed forty days rest.

Once again he was plunged into despair.

'I have decided more than ever,' he announced, 'to give up the bike.' His wife, Bruna, of course, did nothing to help him change his mind. But Fausto quickly recovered his morale and cycle sport smiled on him again.

He won the Grand Prix of Lugano time trial, beating the record for the event. Astrua took second place at more than three minutes; Louison Bobet had to submit to the humiliation of being caught by his rival.

So he found his best form and decided not to give it up. In the middle of the winter season the Grand Prix of the Mediterranean was organised from the 8th to the 17th November. There again nobody could stop him. He carried off the most important stages as well as the final classification.

At the same time, the Campionissimo and Giulia Locatelli actively pursued their correspondence; the doctor's wife managed to get everywhere to see her champion, even in the changing rooms crowded with sweaty riders giving off a smell of embrocation. Nothing stopped her. It was at one of these meetings that she suddenly put it to him:

' You are our friend, why not come to our house at Varano?'

The invitation was formal. Coppi went. Did he not have a nephew doing his military service in the area? An absolutely opportune alibi to explain his trip to people in general and Bruna in particular.

The champion, in spite of his fame and fortune, seemed ill-at-ease. The mistress of the house on the other hand showed herself to be over attentive in her sumptuous lounge. Giulia was beautiful, strangely beautiful in her white linen suit. Straight away she tried to put her guest at his ease.

'I know that you take neither milk or lemon' she said as she served tea.

She had devoted so many hours reading magazine articles on her idol. Consciously or not, Giulia's admiration was already close to resembling love.

This visit brought them closer together, for from then on, Coppi thought of nothing but the young woman, trying hard to be silent about his feelings but in his thoughts, her face kept coming back to him. On another winters' day of the same year, he telephoned the villa, pretending to be passing through the area and offered to visit the Locatelli's. He was welcomed with the same joy as the first time. During the course of the conversation, comfortably installed in the drawing room, he made a suggestion:

'I have been invited to the Sports Palace at Milan to the see the Harlem Globe Trotters, the extraordinary basketball players. A marvellous spectacle. Maybe we can all go together. That particular evening Dr Locatelli still had a large number of consultations. No matter. Fausto and Giulia went to Milan accompanied by a couple of friends, Dr Albrizio and his fiancee Pinuccia. At the last moment Dr Albrizio decided to wait for his associate so Coppi took Giulia and Pinccia.

During the whole of the journey, Fausto appeared radiant. He laughed and joked and was literally transformed and arriving at the Sports Palace wanted only one thing: to be alone next to Giulia. She too had similar designs so it suited them to be rid of their travelling companion. The task was not too arduous in the crowd and the young girl was shaken off.

Both of them watched the show side by side. They were there like two transfixed lovers. Giulia waited for a few words from her companion but he, if he had been articulate a few minutes before, became suddenly and strangely very quiet. He contented himself with looking at Giulia the whole evening, his face lit up with happiness but he was nervous and awkward. Giulia said nothing either. Which of them was the most moved ?

At the exit from the Sports Palace, they came down to earth with a bump, as they came face to face with an impatient Dr Locatelli, who spoke nervously.

'I have been looking for you. I found Pinuccia but not you. You had disappeared. I was ready to think....'

And brusquely Locatelli led Giulia away before she was able to say good-bye and thank him for a lovely evening.

On the way home, the doctor overwhelmed his wife with a whole series of hurtful words. Coppi went down to Novi Ligure. At the wheel of his car he appeared to be very pensive. He had spoken more than normal. Giulia had asked all the questions. She was so beautiful, Giulia and seemed to understand so well. Their eyes had met. He read a deep tenderness in them.

Fausto was moved, simply moved.

At Nova; he was going back to Bruna; Bruna who passed her life at church, Bruna who so often threw in his face: 'I hate your job'.

As he pushed open the door of his villa, he thought that life was unjust. He was looking for other things beside the sweet smell of success.

The Phenomenon

The sports medical centre often received a visit from the Campionissimo. He listened carefully to all the advice that was lavished on him and was always seeking perfection. He searched through the books on dietetics and learned the methods of the famous scientist Gayelord Hauser. Cavanna advised him that the Hauser methods were workable but there were also the theories of other scientists. You had to put them altogether and then apply them to cycling. And this was what Coppi did.

In 1952 Fausto made the acquaintance of Gayelord Hauser, in the lobby of the Hotel Duomo in Milan. The dietician listened to Coppi with great attention and was incredulous to learn that not only had the former peasant from Catellania drawn inspiration from his methods but he had improved on them as well.

All had been very well worked out after careful thought. Each 'menu' was applied to a precise moment, training, recuperation and competition. So what was concluded? that the champion was inspired by the ideas of those 'scientists' of dietetics such as Benedict, Maguers-Levy, Chaveau, Weiss, Kintaro-Oshima...Gayelord Hauser did not come back.

In the morning he took tea accompanied by yoghurt. At the midday meal, he would eat grilled meat, vegetables, fresh fruit and a lot of salad. In the evenings he added wheat germ to his meals and finished them off with herbal tea. Once a week he ate just calves liver and wheat germ. During stage races he often replaced the tea with molasses and by hot sugared orange juice, taken when he woke up. At breakfast time he swallowed a bowl of white coffee with tea and steak with chicken. His food during a race was as follows: ham or honey sandwiches, rice pudding, fruit tarts, oranges, tea, mineral water and fruit juice. As soon as the finishing line was crossed, he refreshed himself with mineral water and an hour later three quarters of a litre of milk.

As far as equipment was concerned, he paid a lot of attention to his bike, for he knew just how much a perfectly assembled machine was worth. He used the services of a skilled and competent man, Pinella de Grandi, who was affectionately known as 'Pinza d'Oro' (golden pliers) who believed that a mechanic should work very closely with a rider. Pinella confided that:

'He is very demanding but the way in which he admires his bicycle each day, with such tenderness, his unique manner of checking it down to the smallest detail, of discovering exactly what I have done, rewards me for all my efforts.

He took three bicycles with him to the start of all the stage races. In this way he always had something suited to the circumstances of the race and the profile of the stages. He was the first to use a lighter bike for time trials and as he wanted the whole cycling community to benefit from his discoveries, he spread the notion of embrocation, of toe clips, of shoes specially designed for competition and even went so far as replacing the model of his sunglasses.

By his very presence and by his advice he incited the Italian manufacturers of bicycles and of equipment to improve, modernise and develop their products. The firms which produced the competition tubular tyres became world famous as much for the quality of their products as for their quantity.

Long sleeve jerseys was another of his brainwaves, the same as jerseys with collars, silk jerseys and racing capes which quickly became regarded to be essential. He redesigned racing hats and track suits which became more elegant and more functional. He studied the problem of wheel covers and ways of protecting spare tubulars, neglecting no detail.

After his arrival at the Tour de France, he revolutionised the habits and customs of the organisation. In 1947 and 1948 riders were expected to make do with a clean jersey every third day and hats were exchanged every fourth day. Everything changed in 1949 with Coppi. His notoriety, the validity of his arguments, led those in charge of the Tour to equip the riders better, so making their life a little easier.

He knew how to prepare for his races and that explains how the Italians were forced to change their ideas, even up to the point of modifying the manner in which they followed the races.

When an attack took place and when a break was formed, the press cars overtook the bunch in order to see how the offensive developed, to evaluate the merits of the attacker and to judge the resistance of the others. With the succession of this Italian phenomenon, this method proved to be irrational. He often took it on himself to decide how the race would be run, to turn it upside down and to make a nonsense of the race timetable. Another phenomenon, one of the most surprising and one which concentrated the attention of the professional followers: when Coppi left the bunch, it meant that the race was over; over for him and for the others. With the punctuality of a civil servant and according to well established process, he left the group and went away beyond the hills and the valleys to victory, even though it might be two hundred kilometres away. This formality became commonplace and this mockery was to last for nine years. There was no exception to the rule, once Coppi had escaped from the pack he was never caught by his pursuers in the period between 1946 and 1954.

Finally, it must be said that the efforts the 'gregarri' made were extraordinary. As a master tactician Coppi pushed his rivals into making mistakes. He thought through each of the races very carefully and tried hard to manoeuvre with the skill of a chess player, placing his lieutenants in a way to cause his adversaries to commit errors, depending on the profile of the land.

His team mates were true athletes with the hard shells of experienced roadmen, capable of the most violent efforts to protect their leader; but also they had heart and souls.

Coppi had a blind confidence in them. In actual fact, for these men, a mere grimace was sufficient to know if a rival was vulnerable or not. They came to warn their chief in the peloton: 'Fausto, now is the moment to attack.'

THE NEW HORIZONS

IN 1953 THE ITALIAN SUPER-CHAMPION RETURNED TO THE TOUR OF ITALY, to confront the Swiss Hugo Koblet again who had already been the winner of this event in 1950 and the Tour de France in 1951. In the time since then, the man from Zurich had known some health problems but seemed to have finally recovered his outstanding form. In spite of a crash in the Abruzze mountains, he retook control of the 'Giro' on the stage from Grossetto to Follonica, run against the watch. It was a real exploit in which he averaged more than forty kilometres an hour, leaving Coppi at almost two minutes.

The Italian champion and all his Bianchi team replied to this success by being victorious in the team time trial stage. Fausto was the one mainly responsible for this win. His men found difficulty in maintaining the pace when it was their turn to lead. 'Bianchi' carried off the stage at an average speed of nearly forty eight kilometres an hour.

However Koblet was still wearing the pink leader's jersey and Coppi followed him at fifty five seconds. The experts thought that the race would be decided on the climbs of the Dolomites and opinions were divided as to the outcome. Coppi was surrounded by a squad containing strong and reliable riders whereas Koblet was practically without team mates; it led most to believe that the Swiss would be rapidly beaten.

Koblet thought it was advisable to dishearten his rivals. In the Vicenza-Auronzo stage, the Swiss went onto the offensive and increased his lead on general classification by a little more than a minute. But anything could still happen on the eighteenth day of the race, between Auronzo and Bolzano, on a road which included the climbs of four major mountains.

Once again Koblet was at the head of the race. The followers were filled with wonder. He was the first over the summit of the Col of Falzarego. Was he going to succeed with this attack? Coppi, of course, wasn't ready to concede defeat, although he had been beginning to doubt himself. When he judged the moment to be right to go and rejoin the elegant Swiss, he embarked upon a remarkable pursuit. The spectacle that ensued was on the same scale as the mountains: grandiose and unreal. You had the impression that it was the pedals which were carrying Coppi who, in just a few kilometres, rejoined the pink jersey, dropped him and crossed alone over the summit of the Col de Sella. The descent led to the finish at Bolzano. But Koblet wasn't finished. Alone he started a 'death defying' descent and rejoined Coppi a few kilometres from the finishing banner.

No doubt, for Coppi, the surprise was scarcely an agreeable one. When the Swiss latched onto his wheel, the Italian said: 'Bravo! You've just won the Giro.'

He had certainly won the stage but was still two minutes behind Koblet on general classification and no longer believed in his chances.

However there remained one final difficulty, the next day, with the climb of the Stelvio which finished two thousand seven hundred and fifty eight metres above sea level and was to be approached from the steep side.

If Coppi no longer believed in his chances, the Bianchi team still did. At the dinner table the tongues loosened. Ettore Milano, one of the 'gregarri' insisted:

'Tomorrow we've got to go up to an altitude of three thousand metres. Koblet weakens at fifteen hundred metres, Fausto, as you know. You've go to try something. You must promise us.'

And the team leader eventually agreed.

At Varano Borghi, Giulia was one of those who believed in and hoped for the final victory of the Campionissimo. Moreover she would be on the slopes of the climb to applaud him. Her husband had promised it. But Dr Locatelli was suffering from a sore throat. In a hard tone he said to his wife:

'If I'm not going, you're not going either. The car will stay here.'

'In that case', she replied, I will get Dr Albizio and Pinuccia to take me!'

All three of them left for the Tour of Italy, crammed into a tiny car with the suitcases taking up most of the room.

The climb had just been opened. In the biting cold Giulia felt as if she was going to die with frozen hands and feet and her teeth chattering. What did it matter, she felt happy, very happy.

In the meantime the riders of this 36th Tour of Italy had left Bolzano for the next stage to Bormio.

At the foot of the Stelvio climb, Andrea Carrea put the plan into operation: to make the race harder. The bunch stretched into one long line. Riders were dropped off the back, one by one. At twelve hundred metres there was still some vegetation but suddenly they all found themselves between two walls of snow.

Coppi did not seem very active, it was as if he was indifferent in spite of the stakes. Then the Bianchi team car drew alongside and Tragella with a red face exhorted him to keep his word.

There were eleven kilometres to the top of the climb. Nine kilometres from the summit, a most moving thing happened: Coppi proudly opened hostilities. Where was Koblet? On the Italian's wheel who in his turn was not in the least bit surprised. All the same, he took note that the Swiss was far less frisky than he had been the previous day. What was going to happen now? Were the two 'greats' going to stop their duel to the summit. No! Coppi got out of the saddle and attacked a second time, a last time...

Koblet pulled a face. He understood. It was over, he would not be winning the Tour of Italy. He watched his adversary draw away with every pedal stroke, smoothly and without any problem. He extended his lead as if he had an engine in his bottom bracket and Koblet, helplessly watched his dream of winning evaporate.

Giulia was waiting, less than five kilometres from the summit. Suddenly two motorcyclists surged round the bend, they were to open up the road for the riders. Behind was a single rider at the head of the race, wearing a sky-blue jersey: Fausto Coppi.

The blue spot started to appear more clearly against the two walls of snow which lined the muddy slippery road.

Fausto accelerated again, with his eyes fixed on a point far in front of him.

By what miracle did he see Giulia? Her white raincoat blended into the snowy background. There are some things which cannot be explained.

Giulia cried out to him:

'Faster Fausto, courage!'

As he drew alongside her the champion found the strength to cry out to her:

'Are you coming to Bormio?'

She shouted back:

'Yes...yes'

But the heavenly blue spot had disappeared. For Giulia and her friends, the descent was even harder than the climb.

When they switched on their little radio, it was to hear: 'So Coppi, in a masterly fashion, has won the pink jersey.'

Giulia burst into tears.

When all three of them arrived at Bormio, it was relatively easy to locate the Bianchi team hotel. The fans were crowding round the entrance. Giulia and her friends wanted to go to Coppi's room but the way was barred by the mechanic Pinella di Grandi.

'Forgive me madam, he said. Only you can go in,'

And Giulia went in and saw Fausto. He was there, wearing a tight-fitting track suit, bearing the name of his bicycle manufacturer. His hair was carefully combed, as if he had just come from the hairdressers, his eyes were sparkling. The young woman thought he looked very handsome.

Fausto came to meet her and for the first time, tried to embrace her. Giulia took a step back:

'Fausto', she said to him laughingly, 'you have won but you must not let the victory turn your head.'

He let her go and then tapping his nose made a sign for her to follow him. This time they were in a corner where no-one could see them. He turned round and said:

'And now, he said, will you give me this kiss? I've won, I've got the jersey, there's no harm in it, it's a victory kiss?'

So this was the way that Giulia and Fausto embraced for the first time. 'A very innocent kiss, the young woman would later say, the kiss of a child.'

On that evening, the night had fallen. It was too late for Giulia and her friends to leave. They decided to spend the night in the Bianchi team hotel. After dinner was over, Fausto got up, left his team mates and joined Giulia at her table. She was alone as her companions had gone off to buy some postcards.

Coppi wanted to speak, there was so much he wanted to say. However he restrained himself. Giulia interrupted the silence:

'You have been very cheerful until the present time. Why have you suddenly become so thoughtful? Aren't you happy? The Tour of Italy is practically finished, you've won...'

He shook his head:

'Yes the Tour is over and I've won. Tomorrow we'll arrive at Milan. After tomorrow there will be the first track meeting at Turin I have to ride. Then, I'll return to Milan. Then I'll go to God knows where. In two weeks time there is a race counting towards the Championship of Italy, then there will be something else. Then I will do the World Championships, then the winter will come, then training and, once again, the Giro...

'Its your life, I think you get enough satisfaction from it all to make you happy. You want everything...'

'That's what you believe, but you're on the outside. Being feted as a champion, the sport, the victories, the medals, Paris, Brussels, the people clapping. Of course you put some money by. Of course you make a fortune, you imagine you're making a fortune...'

'Yes but if you have nothing behind you, why do you risk breaking you're bones for nothing? Haven't you got a house, a family, friends? It certainly seems to me as if you have...'

Coppi shrugged his shoulders.

'I've got nothing, I don't know why I'm doing it at all. I don't know for who I'm doing it. No, I've got nobody. Nobody...'

What Fausto told Giulia that evening, was strange, antagonising. Their two destinies met and mingled. The supporter of the champion who was number one in the world became aware that he felt alone, sadly alone and without any hope, although he was a star who triumphed when he decided to do so.

The day following the Stelvio stage, the Tour of Italy came to an end at the Vigorelli at Milan. Coppi had won his fifth Giro. His margin was minimal, only one minute and twenty nine seconds. He was thirty four years old. From that time on he knew that his sporting days were numbered. So he would have to be careful. He had never been able to win the World Championships on the road. This time he was going to devote himself to achieving this goal. The event took place at Lugano on the 30th August on a circuit which was perfectly suited to him. In order to prepare for it properly, he renounced the Tour de France. In actual fact at his age the Tour of Italy and the Tour de France were not advisable in the same year,

At Milan, at the finish of the Giro, Giulia Locatelli rejoined him. She was there amongst the anonymous crowd pressed against the fencing in front of the stands. With the others she shouted the name of Fausto, and he, as if by a miracle, heard her. He looked towards the stands, saw her, and extricating himself from the circle of people who surrounded him, got on his bike, then, slowly, started to ride round the exterior of the wooden track. He fixed his eye on her so that he would not lose her from view and approached her. Dr Locatelli who was accompanying her, waved his hand in salute.

The winner of the Tour of Italy arrived at the metal grill and held onto it with a finger. He held out his right hand to them. Giulia realised that he had slipped a piece of paper into her hand. She closed her fist and quickly slipped it into the pocket of her suede jacket. Then as usual she went down to the changing rooms.

Fausto was getting dressed after having showered. He arrived knotting his tie. Dr Locatelli was replying to the greeting of a friend outside, Fausto leaned towards Giulia to whisper to her:

'Please do...

'What?' She replied. 'What are you talking about?'

'The paper? Haven't you looked at it?'

She had no time to reply. The doctor arrived from behind. It was only when she was back at the house at Varano that she could at last read the nine word message: 'Tomorrow at four o'clock, at Tortona, at the station.

This time the young woman did not try to resist their destiny. She left the house on the pretext of a 'fitting' for Pinuccia's wedding.

At the station among the crowd, Giulia straight away recognised the faithful Giovanni Chiesa. He had come to meet her and said simply to her: 'Fausto is waiting for you.'

He immediately took her, by car, to a destination that she did not know. They left Tortona, passing through the villages of Villalvernia, Cassano-Spinola and stopped just before Novi Ligure at the exact spot where the motorway to Serravalle began. There, in front of an electrical transformer, a grey car was parked. Inside was Fausto Coppi. Chiesa left her there and went away.

Inside the car, the two of them felt intimidated and embarrassed, pre-occupied by everything they had to say to each other, because they wanted to say it. No sound, no words came out of their mouths. Everything appeared so strange...

Did they understand what was happening in their hearts, in their souls, during this rendez-vous of silence?

Fausto, after a certain time, took her by the hand and tried to kiss her, surreptitiously, but without insisting as if he was waiting to be rebuffed. Finally it was he who interrupted the long silence.

'Thank you for coming to Tortona. I understand that the way I fixed this meeting was a little unusual...But I did not know what else to do.

'There are so many things that we do without really thinking about why we do them, Giulia replied. I didn't know why I made this journey here,'

Then, brusquely, Fausto said to her:

'Of course I must say something to you. Of course you're waiting for me to speak.

'Obviously Fausto, but it's very difficult...If we feel attracted to each other...But I'm not a woman who can allow herself to have an adventure. Fausto, I have two children. The Locatelli couple soon after giving birth to a girl, had a second child, a boy called Maurizio.'

So the conversation continued slowly, with painful pauses. Giulia and Fausto said practically nothing.

Soon it was time to catch the train to take her back home. Chiesa took her back to the station. On the way back Giulia was overcome with melancholy.

Sacred Lugano

THE SUMMER OF 1953 ARRIVED, RADIANT AND SPLENDID.

So Coppi did not ride the Tour de France in order to concentrate on his main objective: the World Road Championship.

By way of preparation, for the first part of the programme that he had fixed for himself, he chose France. He had arranged to ride a few criteriums before training on the Alpine roads. So he took advantage of it to greet the riders of the Tour de France, on the slopes of the Iozard, for example. Three men - three faithful ones - accompanied him: Carrea, Milano and Gaggero. The journey also permitted Fausto to get away from Italy where the press severely criticised his non-participation in the Tour.

The thoughts of the Campionissimo were concentrated on Giulia. It was her and only her, who, from then, haunted his days and his nights. The young woman too was confused and she decided to take a step back. She had gone to stay with her aunt Dina, at Sinigalla, on the Adriatic, in order to take advantage of the sea and the sun.

One morning, Coppi again showed his impatience. He called her on the telephone. He said to her briefly:

'I'll wait for you tomorrow at Tortona. Don't forget your passport. We're going away.'

He did not say more, no doubt fearing that she would refuse. Nevertheless she asked herself: where is he taking me? Why do I need a passport?

During the greater part of the day, she could not make up her mind, weighing things up, turning her thoughts in one direction and then the other. Finally she went to her aunt and said that she had to go to Varano urgently.

At Tortona station, Giovanni Chiesa was again waiting for her. He gave her the keys to Coppi's car and then left in another car with his team mates - after explaining the route to Clavieres, a little village on the frontier between Italy and France, where she was awaited.

A few hours later after she had driven up the Col de Montgenevre, at the summit near Clavieres, her heart started to beat faster. Here she was face to face with Fausto. Her face turned crimson and Coppi blushed with her. As on previous occasions, conversation proved difficult.

'How beautiful you are, so brown...'

They made preparations to pass through the frontier post into France. In front of the customs men, she opened her bag to get her passport out. She nervously hunted for it, turning everything out. Unfortunately she had forgotten it, it was still at Ancona.

In his gentle voice he reassured her:

'Don't worry. I'll go and see the officials. I think that they know me and trust me.'

He smiled. Giulia saw him chatting with an officer. Obviously the discussion was a good-natured one. He returned with a pass.

'I've got it, he told her, but I had to tell a lie. I said that you were my wife. What else could I do?'

In France a little hotel welcomed them. Fausto had already booked a room.

This time he had thought things over carefully. Sure of himself, he spoke slowly but firmly:

'I have made my choice. You must not leave me anymore. I want you always to be at my side.

'And what about Lolli and Maurizo?' she replied. 'They are my children.'

'I too, have thought about them. Of course it's very hard. But many people take the risk of getting divorced and remarrying. We'll do the same and you will keep the two children with you.'

'Everyone will be against me.'

'No matter. I have weighed that up as well. I will not let you leave again.'

For several long hours, they planned their future together. they were happy, alone in the world. Fausto said to her again in a gentle voice:

'It's decided. You'll come everywhere with me.'

Soon the 22nd July 1953 dawned after a long night which had just sealed two destinies. A new road opened out in front of them, sown with perils and marked out with intolerance.

They went to the Col d'Izoard as planned, where the Tour de France was passing by under a magnificent sun. The road was swarming with people. They settled down at the start of the section known as the 'Casse Deserte', a sort of lunar landscape planted with monolithic blocks. A scene worthy of the Tour.

The first rider arrived. He was alone in the lead. It was his friend Louison Bobet. Fausto had brought his camera and was enjoying himself taking photos. Then as they came through he waved at and encouraged

126

the men he rubbed shoulders with so often.

Suddenly a press photographer discovered Coppi, called his colleagues and the two lovers found themselves literally encircled and blinded by dozens of flash bulbs.

At the time they scarcely paid attention to all the commotion around them. But a few days later the photos appeared in the newspapers. At Varano Borghi, one kind soul took one of them to Dr Locatelli:

'Tell me, isn't that your wife there?'

When Giulia returned to Ancona, a very severe letter was waiting for her from her husband; it was at the same time full of questions, supplications and menaces.

It seemed that the moment had not come for either to burn the bridges or to put their cards on the table. It took all her imagination to think up an excuse for being at the Tour de France. It consisted of, according to her version of the facts, of a coach excursion, organised by one of their friends, a former rider, Ubaldo Pugnaloni, who really did live in Ancona. Once there, by the purest of chance, she met Coppi.

Did Locatelli believe this story? Nobody knows. When she left Ancona for Verano she was met with a very cold welcome indeed, but without a scene.

Nevertheless she could no longer put up with him, and having to stay at home, far from the one she now loved so much. She rejoined him at Lugano, in Switzerland, where the World Championships were taking place and on which Coppi had staked everything. When she crossed the frontier the crowd was ecstatic. The fans had come to see their God: Coppi.

The Italian Champion was in a particularly good mood. The day before, his protégé Ricardo Filippi had carried off the world amateur title. A good omen.

Having been on the spot for several weeks, he had had many outings with team mates and young riders who were under the wing of Biago Cavanna. He had placed all these men several times, as hares, on a climb and being the last, set off to catch them. The times that he achieved and the ease with which he caught them indicated, day after day, how far his preparation and his form had progressed. Coppi and his companions got up each day at six o'clock. They trained in exactly the same conditions as they would race in, noting all details of the profile of the event, getting used to riding in the heat of the day and choosing their gears with care.

Cavanna, for his part, prepared on the day of the race, a bottle of pure caffeine which must have had an extraordinary effect on Coppi.

Three hundred thousand fans packed the circuit. On the start line Cavanna was deeply anxious.

'Let's hope that all goes well for Fausto, he confided. Do you know

Coppi photographs Bobet at the Tour de France 1953. Beside him, the 'White Lady'

Meeting in secret. Coppi and the 'White Lady' at a cabaret in Milan, 1953

he has the intention of making me go to a clinic, close to here, so that I could have an operation on my eyes. Well I can tell you that if I was asked today: 'What would you sooner have most? To recover sight or for Coppi to win? 'I wouldn't hesitate for a second. I would prefer to give up my sight so that Fausto could become World Champion.'

Giulia was at the circuit.

From the very first kilometres, the young Luxemburger Charly Gaul opened the hostilities. He was to remain in front for almost half of the race. Then the best men took their place at the front. This was the moment that Coppi chose to go away alone. Kubler and Bobet were a little way ahead. He rejoined Kubler first before bringing back Bobet and continuing his fine solitary effort. But the Belgian Derycke succeeded in getting onto his wheel. Coppi's domination began. Geminiani later spoke of a hallucination:

'I saw him take off like a rocket. I tried hard to react and even got within a few metres of his wheel. But Fausto had gone away with prestigious strength. He dropped all the group, taking two hundred metres out of Bobet and myself in half a kilometre! It was perhaps the greatest surprise of my career. Never did I see that again!'

For seventy kilometres, the Italian and the Belgian stayed together, with Coppi doing most of the work. With two laps to go, the brave Derycke showed signs of weakening.

Giulia stayed close to the finishing line. 'Commandatore' Zambrini, director general of Bianchi, saw her and quickly took her by the arm and placed her at the front in full view of Coppi so as to lend the Italian more strength.

Fausto did see her. He threw all his strength into an attack and Derycke was dropped for good.

Coppi became World Champion. For a long time he cried in the arms of Biagio Cavanna. His joy increased when the directors of the International Cycling Union put the rainbow jersey on him and he found Giulia who had come to the podium as well. She held back her tears but her emotion was genuine. The flash bulbs spluttered. In Italy the next day the photo of Coppi the adulterer appeared. He was certainly Champion of the World but he was not at the end of his worries and his misfortune.

Today the crowd cried but tomorrow it turned against him and Giulia was shouted down as the 'sinner' who too quickly meddled in the life of 'their champion'.

Some journalists, however, did not want to believe it and in glowing terms reported only the fine success which he had brought to the cycling world. In 'Lo Sport' could be read:

'Today again there are ill-intentioned people of bad faith, who are affirming the most stupid and unbelievable things. Let us stop this

World Champion, Lugano, 1953

The photo that scandalised puritanical Italy. The ' White Lady' with Coppi at the World Championships ceremony

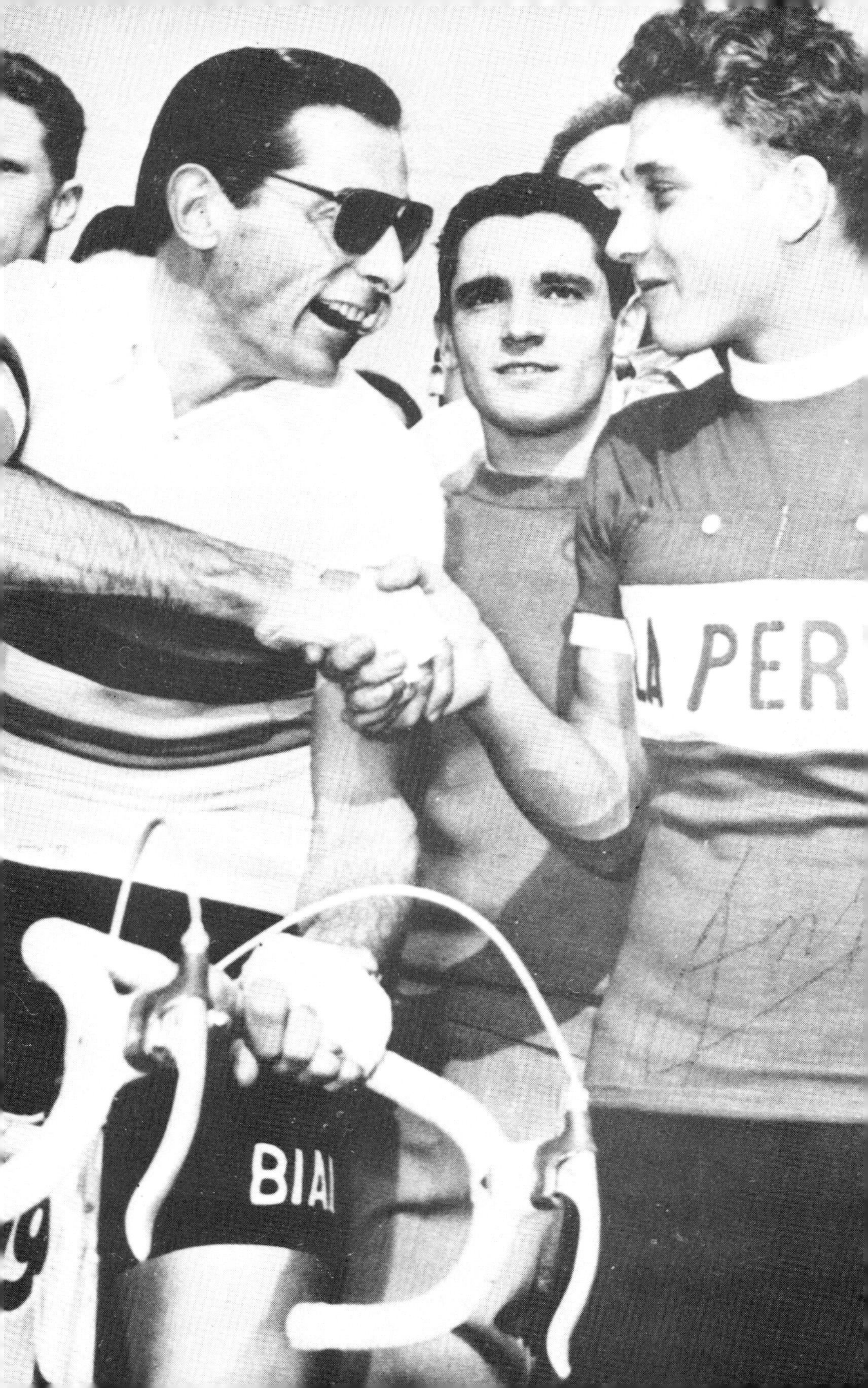
LA PER
BIA

campaign of calumny and raise up this superb athlete, who had given us such great joy. Let us raise Coppi up, let us all raise up our sport and this dear bicycle which, in spite of everything, still represents our passion and our victory.'

One has the impression that Fausto remained insensitive to all the uproar. From now on he wanted to make his life with Giulia and nobody was going to stop him. All of the world had to know it.

In an interview on the Italian radio, the new World Champion concluded with:

'...I am really am very happy; I embrace my mother and Marina.'

Bruna no longer existed for him.

To Raphael Geminiani he confided:

'I am madly in love, like a kid. I am ready to make a fool of myself. Whatever happens will happen. It's just good to be alive.'

And Coppi continued, as if the critics were of no concern to him. A rainbow jersey was not enough for him. He wanted the title of 'King of the Pursuiters' and did not hesitate to challenge the holder of the world champion's jersey at this speciality: the Australian Sid Patterson. The world title was not a stake but the prestige was. In the month of May, Coppi had already beaten the Australian, who at this time had prepared very well for revenge.

The encounter was fixed for the 4th September at the Vigorelli in Milan which was sold out for this match between the world road Champion and the world track champion.

On paper Patterson was favourite. He was the real specialist. However from the first laps, one could see an over excited Coppi lifted by the crowd. From start to finish he dominated the Australian to finally realise his best-ever time in a pursuit, 6'06": an average speed of 49.1353 kph. It was a brutal lesson for Patterson.

Finally, the Baracchi Trophy came round. The event which traditionally closed the season, Coppi was partnered by the Amateur world champion, Ricardo Filippi. This time it was the event record that was broken. The two world champions triumphed at an average of 43.713 to bring a remarkable season to a close.

The Lady in White

FOR COPPI, GLORY WAS WITHOUT DOUBT A MARVELLOUS THING BUT HE HAD ALWAYS VIEWED IT WITH A CERTAIN AMOUNT OF APPREHENSION. He who was an astonishingly warm human being, never really saw himself as a great star. On the contrary he thought that he should and could live like everyone else. However, for Italy, Coppi was a symbol. He was a national hero and an example. As such he had to show himself to be incorruptible.

Coppi, on the contrary, only wanted to be himself, to live with those he loved. He forgot that a champion no longer belonged only to himself.

He dreamed only of Giulia in spite of all the attempts to make him return to his legitimate wife. He did go back but not for very long. As far as Giulia was concerned her husband knew the truth but still pretended to ignore it all; for the couple the atmosphere was unbearable. In Italy the press still maintained the 'mystery'.

Coppi needed to breath the air of the green countryside which he had known since his childhood, and from where he had come to find fame and fortune. At the beginning of October, a short time after having won the 'supreme' title at Lugano, he decided to take Giulia to Castellania. They thought that there, they could get away from the scandal.

With an infinite tenderness, he looked at the valley stretching out before his eyes, after having passed through villages whose names were like music to his ears: Cerezzano-Superiore, Paderna etc.

The world champion and his companion pushed open the great worm-eaten door to his families home. Mother Angiolina. She knew nothing of her son's liaison. At Castellania, had the children got wind of what certain papers were saying? It seemed as if they had said nothing to 'mamma'. At least, if they had done, she would have swept all these stories away with a wave of her hand. She trusted her Fausto. Anyway she appeared quite intimidated before this great beautiful and distinguished lady. So few elegant people were seen in this quiet corner of the world.

The World Champion talks to
some school children in
Castellania.

Coppi and his aunt Albina
at the school where he
learnt to read

Coppi with the village bus drivers of Castellania

Coppi as world champion riding the 3rd stage St-Etienne-Vergèze in Paris Nice, 1954

Fausto showed Giulia around the house. He took her to a lumber room.

'Look, he said to her,' opening a refrigerator. 'I gave it to her a few months ago. She has never plugged it in. She puts her dirty washing in it. I have never had the heart to scold her...'

They walked back up the street, the visit was over. There was a special light breeze blowing which made the brown leaves rustle. He felt at home in this peaceful village far from any bustle. The peasants were working in the fields. A long way off a dog was barking and it was echoing off the hills. The two of them breathed the happiness of being together. But not for long.

All his youth flashed before Coppi's mind. He seemed troubled and Giulia seemed more moved than he did. This visit to Castellania made their troubles worse. They knew that the road to their salvation would be long, very long. Perhaps they were not completely conscious of it. 'Love is blind' as the saying went. For them, however, nobody had the right to vilify a great passion, even if it was illegal or against the laws of church.

Giulia claimed she would move mountains if she had to.

The problems did not stop Fausto, on the 4 th March 1954, from starting the season victoriously, in Sardinia, by winning the Circuit of Cagliari, unleashing the enthusiasm of the ten thousand spectators present. It was a good pointer to form for him as he lined up for the Paris-Nice race.

It was necessary to honour his world champion's jersey. In the third stage, Nice-Vergeze he followed a brusque attack by Lucien Teisseire, four kilometres from the finish. He caught the man and won the stage under torrential rain.

Victory again in the Tour of Campania, in Italy Fausto was the best man at the beginning of the season.

When he lined up for the start of the Tour of Italy, he was the man to beat. In fact on the first day, he took the leader's pink jersey. Unfortunately, on the second day, he suffered from stomach pains and finished a long way down and considered that he had already lost the Giro.

Every evening he and Giulia phoned each other; she from Giavirate and places close to home, he from the stage town.

Coppi was happy, but resigned as far as the Giro was concerned. He did not consider that it was his concern to do all the work at the front of the race. If the others wanted to win then it was up to them. He had no desire to pull the chestnuts out of the fire for the rest of them. As a consequence, at the end of the sixth stage at Aquila, the Swiss Clerici - accompanied by the Italian Guido Assirelli - came in forty minutes in front of all the stars. It is hardly necessary to say that with such a lead

Fausto and Giulia want to be private but.......

Tour of Italy 1954 : Coppi, Koblet and Astrua escaping on the Col l'Abetone

the Swiss roadmen had already won the race, even if there were still fifteen days to go.

The more the days went past, the more Coppi appeared to be tormented. His only aim was to see Giulia no matter what. He made a rendez-vouz with her at Riva del Garda, one of the stage towns. He was no longer himself. He finished only second on the time trial stage behind Hugo Koblet on the road around Lake Garda, was he losing his form?

He was pursued in his private life. His morale seemed to be effected. He was booed. The spectators whistled and shook their fists. He felt uneasy. In the evenings after the stages, Biagio Cavanna was there to restore the 'motor'. Gently feeling the legs of which he knew every fibre, endeavouring to soothe the worried soul as he relaxed the rebellious muscles.

'It's in the Dolomites that you will demonstrate that you are still Coppi. You have lost this Giro but even you still need to show that you are the greatest. It is not enough to break up the race, to make the others try to follow you while in a panic. You must produce something really special to prove that Coppi is still the Campionissimo.'

Giulia arrived. She had managed to get away from her husband on the pretext that she had to visit a friend urgently at Urgano.

In the caravan of the Tour of Italy, the news of the presence of Coppi's 'friend' spread like wildfire and the radio spoke of nothing else. They had resolved their problems and there was no going back, not that they wanted to.

The next day, she crossed the frontier into Switzerland and went to St Moritz where the Giro stopped on the penultimate day of the race.

In the meantime Coppi seemed to have found his best form. The day before the 'Swiss' stage between St Martino-di-Castrozzo and Bolanzo, the Campionissimo could be seen in a 'state of grace'. On the Climb of the Pordoi, nobody could resist him. It was 'his' day in the chain of the Dolomites where he showed the full value of his elegant pedalling action. He won alone, at Bolzano, where a delirious crowd greeted him. They had forgotten their rancour.

The Italian champion rehabilitated? Not for long. The next day between Bolanzo and St Moritz a scandal erupted. The riders decided to go on strike, riding at twenty kilometres and hour and crossing the Col of Bernina in one big group, something never seen before. One will never know exactly who pushed the riders into such an action. All that can be said for sure is most of the newspapers accused Coppi of being the instigator.

Form that moment on the Campionissimo was the target for the French newspaper L'Equipe. An entire page was devoted to slinging mud at him. They even dared, in a column on the front page, to attack his private life.

138

'It is obvious,' read the article on the 14th June 1954, 'that in sporting circles everything is known about the Campionissimo's change of life. A change which is hardly compatible with the demands of the profession of a champion.

It is not our place to interfere in the private life of anyone, unless it explains his actions.

Then, under the title 'Coppi is going to miss his exit' Jacques Goddet wrote one of the most violent diatribes of his career, of which the following is an extract:

'If, Fausto, you have not even taken the trouble to take away the position of the first Italian from the modest Assirelli (in 3rd place overall) in the mountains, if you have entered into this unsavoury game of a strike, if you have cheated the public who had been waiting for you since the early morning at two thousand three hundred metres to see you get your revenge, it is a poor declining Campionissimo, you were afraid. Afraid of suffering, afraid of being able to dominate or of collapsing , afraid of disappointing.

He is no longer mentally or physically capable of sustaining an effort, the repetition of the effort, or even the idea of a struggle. He has become a haunted person where the ghosts of past exploits jostle together, in an awful way, with the pursuit of sacks of guineas which have become so swollen that they have become crushing burdens.

Coppi finished this Giro as a shamefully bad loser. He came out of it insulted, struck down, disparaged, as a man branded as the cholera of international cycling. It remains for him to stop him totally corrupting the sport now that the state of crisis has been revealed.'

What was the sense of these inadmissible attacks? The reply could be found with the recent arrival of the so called 'extra-sportif' groups which were new to cycling and later to be known as 'sponsors'.

The first to adhere to the new movement was, in 1954, Fiorenzo Magni, who wore the colours of Nivea beauty cream. What was Coppi going to do? On his attitude could depend the success or failure of this survival attempt for cycle sport. For that is what it really was; Italian riders perhaps more than French ones were in danger of being unemployed, Italian manufacturers no longer having the means to equip them.

It has to be admitted that Coppi could easily have taken no interest in the affair. If he was indifferent to other riders leaving the sport, he had the means to remain neutral. Or he could support Magni and his Nivea team mates.

This is what was at the heart of the story.

Coppi discovered intolerance everywhere.

His troubles were not over.

At St Moritz, when he crossed the finishing line of the stage, Giulia was there dressed in a white raincoat. The journalists saw her embracing Coppi. One of them Luigi Boccaccini, wrote the next day in the columns of his journal 'La Stampa', 'La Dama in biancho di Fausto Coppi'. The personality of the 'White Lady' was born. A few months later, another journalist Beppe Pegolotti, a native of Florence and a staunch Bartali supporter poured out still more in this sentimental drama by supplying more details in the newspaper. 'Il Carlino della Nazione'. Puritanical Italy refused to believe this incredible alliance between the gentlemen and the adventuress.

The next morning, the 'White Lady' returned to Varano. Her husband was still in bed. By the side of him the newspapers were piling up, in every sense. All of them clearly evoked the liaison of Fausto Coppi with the young lady of Varano Borghi, the wife of a doctor. Photos of the world championships at Lugano, which showed the two lovers side by side, reappeared.

Locatelli made no gesture.

It was over. Giulia took off her bracelet, the symbol of her legal alliance, and put it in a box. Like a robot she opened her wardrobe and took out a suitcase. Into it she put some handkerchiefs, some trousers and left the house.

Roughly one hundred and fifty kilometres separated Varano and Tortona. During the journey, the 'White Lady' experienced the worst torments. The idea of going back came into her head but was quickly replaced by the ardent will to continue.

Fausto, for his part, went to his villa and packed his cases. He left nothing with Bruna to remind her of cycling...

Bobet and Coppi at the Parc des Princes. Behind Raymond Le Bert, Bobet's soigneur

The Wanderers

All of Italy refused to have anything to do Fausto Coppi. In many families it was from now on forbidden to even mention his name. In schools his photos, which adorned the walls, were taken down. But even worse, they were replaced with ones of his rival Bartali.

Where would they set up home? At Tortona, Giovanni Chiesa had rented a little apartment for them, but when the owners found out that the 'White Lady' was there, they had to move everything out on the same night. The persecution had begun.

At Castelleto d'Orba, a few kilometres away, they settled into a rather comfortable and welcoming hotel; Castelleto d'Orba, the name rang in Fausto's ears. In actual fact, it was in this area, in 1938, that he won his first race.

But life at the hotel quickly became unbearable, as they were at the mercy of certain journalists, who harassed them unceasingly.

A fine house came on the market at Novi Ligure, on the road to Seravalle, at a place known as Barbelotta. It was the Villa Carla, flanked by pergolas and venetian lanterns.

The first time she saw it, the young woman did not like it. To her the house appeared cold, austere and dilapidated. But Fausto encouraged her, they would be able to transform it, to make it brighter and more habitable.

But the Italian champion, once again, was struck by misfortune.

On the 7th July, while he was riding in company with Ettore Milano on the road near to Pavia, he suddenly became aware of a lorry. Suddenly the spare wheel fell off the vehicle and struck Coppi. The champion collapsed. His head hit the road. It was later discovered that he had a fractured skull.

He was in a hurry to confront the public. The doctors recommended a long rest. He did not listen to them. Scarcely had the bandages been removed from his head than he was back on his bicycle.

He was expecting to be greeted with enthusiasm, saluting his recovery. For the first time he was whistled and booed. Between the

142

champion, miraculously saved, and his second wife, the Italian public had chosen.

He triumphed at the time of his re-entry into competition, before the world road championships. In the Tour of Switzerland, although he was a little more than a convalescent, he carried off the second stage, at Davos.

Exhausted and out of breath by the effort he had produced, he leant towards Biagio Cavanna and murmured:

'This time they won't whistle me.'

At that same instant, in the middle of the Swiss crowd, an Italian cried out:

'Stay with your wife, Fausto!'

Then Coppi went away towards the showers, with his head lowered. In spite of his refound talent, in spite of his victory, his compatriots would nor forgive him.

Pope Pius XII intervened. The president of the Italian National Sports Centre, Bartolo Paschetta, in a letter addressed to him on the 8th July 1954, wrote: 'Dear Fausto, yesterday evening St Peter made it known to me that the news had caused him a lot of pain...'

Fausto rolled the letter into a ball and threw it away.

The second stage of the Tour of Switzerland was not his only success. He also won the time trial run over ninety eight kilometres which separated Lecco from Lugano. The Italian Pasquale Fornara, in second place, was relegated to nearly five minutes and could hardly believe it. He asked for the result sheets to be verified, an involuntary but now eloquent exercise to the sovereignty of 'faustissimo'.

From that moment on, the 'Coppi complex' reappeared in this peloton composed of mainly Italian riders. They even confirmed the fact that they intended to use all their strength to dethrone this illustrious champion who once again condescended to leave them only in part of the cake. To him it was the better part as for Coppi the Tour of Switzerland was just a step on the road to recovery and he contented himself with two stage wins and the climbers title.

Fausto wanted a divorce, to break the links which united him to Bruna. Italy had sworn to stop him. At the time divorce did not exist in this part of Italy. The emissaries that he had sent to the Vatican came back with a flea in the ear. The cardinals who had received them were formal: the Vatican is not the Bicycle Union. The refused to budge. Marriage is not redundant.

So Italy reproached him for his behaviour. Soon it saw a sign. Burglars broke into the 'Villa Coppi' and stole the fine clothes of the champion.

'The punishment begins! could be read from here and there.

However, at the beginning of this Autumn, the two lovers thought they could hope for some rest, some new, more intimate happiness, something more complete. They gave the impression of a happy couple in spite of all the fury unleashed against them.

Everything was peaceful. The heavy bronze gates sealed them off. Tilde - a little young brunette who acted as a servant, had been dismissed by Dr Locatelli - had been taken back into service by her mistress. She had locked the door securely and went up the stairs to put out this lights.

In the garden, the poplars, the blue firs and the maple trees, nodded gently under the caresses of a light wind as they made a singing noise. A night just like the other had begun; or at least that was they had thought.

It was close to midnight. Somebody rang at the big gates. Tilde was the first up. She switched on the exterior light and went out. She came back upset.

'Madam, she said, it's Dr Locatelli, with the police. They want to come into the Villa.'

Giulia left the bedroom that she shared with Fausto, threw a dressing gown over her night-dress and went downstairs. Rapidly she went to another bedroom with a wardrobe full of her clothes and slipped into bed.

During this time, Dr Locatelli had come into the garden, remained a certain distance from the house and shouted insults at the woman who was still his wife in the eyes of the law. With him was one of his friends, Dr Albrizzo. It was a tiresome and sickening scene. He overwhelmed her with horrible accusations and likened her to a prostitute.

Soon he became bolder and approached the house. In the meantime, Fausto had come downstairs. Hearing Dr Locatelli's screams, he went into the garden to stop him.

'This is my house', he said to his companion. 'I am going to throw this individual into the road.'

'Fausto. I beg you, calm down. Stay there', Giulia cried to him.

The men approached each other. A man in uniform, a brigadier in the police, was in front of the door. He spoke sharply to the young maid:

'Madam Giulia Occhini, does she live here? Where is she?'

The room was pointed out on the ground floor. The brigadier went straight there, knocked on the door, entered, glanced around the room and without saying a word opened a wardrobe. Then he said at the top of his voice:

'No men's clothes!'

He went away to inspect Fausto's bedroom. After having stopped for a while, he noted the existence of the big bed and of two ruffled pillows.

'Are you sleeping alone in this room?' he asked the champion. 'If so why have you got a double bed?'

'I am like a lot of my colleagues', Coppi replied. 'We like to sleep in a big bed to stretch out our legs. That way you get more rest.'

The enquiry was over. What was going to happen next? All hope of living in peace disappeared once again as the police left the house. Fausto took Giulia in his arms and pressed her closely to him. They both stayed like that for a while without moving. A few minutes later Coppi recovered his composure; Giulia said she was prepared to face up to the world if necessary.

The next day Coppi left Italy to honour a contract at the Sports Palace in Brussels. Giulia stayed alone without daring to leave the confines of the garden. At Novi Ligure everyone turned their back on her. Some overexcited people might even spit in her face and who knows - in this town of 35,000 inhabitants, situated on the road to Genoa, she could find herself face to face with Bruna Ciampolini, the 'wife' of her lover. She remained fenced in. Tilde brought her rumours from the city and the newspapers, who had now learned everything. Two days later, in fact, she could read in 'La Stampa' that Dr Locatelli had denounced her for adultery and leaving the conjugal home.

Following this plaint, Fausto and Giulia were constrained to stay in Italy and surrender their passports.

For Coppi the withdrawal of this document meant that he was obliged to cancel some lucrative contracts. He nevertheless put up with this vexation with the greatest of calm. Never did Giulia hear him complain of the humiliation to which he was submitted.

Italy in this year of 1954 seemed to revel in all the scandals which were served up to them by a certain type of press. The ghost of a dead woman relaunched this type of affair. It was the 'Affair Wilma Montesi'. This young woman of 22, a remarkable beautiful brunette had been discovered a year previously on the deserted beach of Torre Vainica, near to Istia, a few kilometres from Rome. The case was quickly closed but a journalist, Silvano Muto, director-founder of the review 'Attualita' relaunched the enquiry as it appeared to him to contain many obscure points. According to him - who had become the Emile Zola of this Italian Dreyfus Affair - the enquiry, conjured away by the police, was nothing other than the conclusion of a series of forbidden pleasures in which members of Italian high society were involved.

'The Coppi Affair' was meat and drink to many Italians and helped the 'scandal sheets' to maintain large circulation's.

There was nothing scandalous about the case. It was just a story of the heart, almost banal. The drama which called into question the 'God' of Italy, tried hard to see love triumph. The road was full of pitfalls. The Italian laws were almost inescapable.

Solid as a Rock

THERE WAS NO LET-UP IN THE PERSECUTION.

One evening, once again the bell rang at the big garden gates. A captain of the police demanded entry.

Giulia and Fausto received him on the steps, brought him into the living room and invited him to sit down. He refused in a polite but firm way and asked the mistress of the house to come with him to help with his investigation.

At Alessandria - the main administrative area for Novi Ligure - the police car drove her to a district where she had never before been. It stopped in front of a large building with heavily bolted doors.

She got out of the car and suddenly understood everything. She had been taken to prison. The gate opened and then closed behind her and the police captain. From now on everything was clear. Shown into an austere office, she found herself in front of one who seemed to be the director of the penitentiary establishment. The interrogation consisted of one simple question:

'Madam, you must think it all over. If you return to Varan Borghi, to your husband's house, we will have nothing more to do with you.'

The sentence had hardly fallen from the lips of the man, when Giulia Locatelli, without giving a moment's reflection, looked him straight in the face and said in a strong voice:

'I am not giving in!"

From there she was led into the main office. She was submitted to another interrogation and replied in the same manner, without a moment's hesitation. Searched and then stripped, she was finally led to her cell.

As she entered it, in the darkness, she was aware that it was already occupied. She breathed in human odours. At the end of the cell, a window showed a square of sky. She understood the rumours of the town, of the people outside. With horror she realised she had been thrown in with common prisoners.

The hours passed, the sky grew pale. Soon the sun would be coming up. Giulia did not even doze. From then on she figured out her new and tiny universe. Four beds, four chairs, four women, herself included. Her other cell companions were curled up under the blankets. When they woke up they wanted to know who she was and why she was in prison.

By standing on tiptoe she could just get a view of the corner of the square, from the window. In this corner a car passed and repassed, the vehicle looked familiar, it was Fausto's. Of course he could not see his companion but his presence reassured her.

Fausto, for his part, had not given up. but his efforts with the prison authorities had no great effect. On the other hand, from the very first day he was able to send food into Giulia, brought from the very best shops in town. But she had no strength to eat it and left it for the other prisoners.

During four days and four nights in prison, her only consolation was the pleasure of seeing Fausto not leave the square. On the morning of the fifth day, the door opened. She was led to the director's office in a state of extreme exhaustion.

'You're free', he said to her. 'There is only one restriction. The judge, taking account of your condition, orders you to stay in Ancona with members of your family. You will have to reside at Ancona. Every Sunday you will be obliged to present yourself at the police station, to sign the register.'

Coppi accompanied her to the shores of the Adriatic with all the other riders of the Bianchi team. They installed themselves in a hotel at Portonovo, where the view of the sea was magnificent. The summer was just coming to an end and you could still bathe. Fausto and his men raced at the velodromes and in the criteriums. He returned, at night, at the wheel of his car to be with Giulia again. Both of them were in love, young and enthusiastic.

It was during this period, a happy and sad one, that Giulia became certain that she was expecting a child. The month of September came to a close. The Autumn had arrived. Fausto learned the news in the middle of a stormy night when he returned from a criterium at Padova.

'I don't feel well, she said to him, but we must rejoice: I am going to have your child. A son, our son! We'll call him Fausto like you.'

This event, so much waited for, appeared to bring them happiness. Fausto forgot his torments and it was almost in a state of euphoria that he started the Tour of Lombardy. He had just celebrated his thirty fifth birthday. If he was no longer in his first youth he possessed an accomplished sense of experience. It was going to serve him well. It really refuted those who had already 'buried' him.

Under an incessant rain, on small roads in poor condition, he controlled the race from the start, letting only those escape who seemed of no real danger, while patiently waiting for the major difficulty of the day: the difficult climb of the Madonna del Ghisallo. Here he was to be seen launching himself into a violent pursuit of two young professionals: Aldo Moser and Chiarlone. He joined them and dropped them.

There remained fifty kilometres to the finish at Milan. But Coppi found himself rejoined by a group of nine men. It was a point of honour to beat them in the sprint - he did.

He continued to ride on the track. In the Sports Palace at Milan on the 27th November he met world champion Louison Bobet over three matches and beat him. On the fourth of November, he carried off the Baracchi Trophy partnered again with Ricardo Fillipi, beating the Bobet-Anquetil team. In the last thirty kilometres Coppi alone led from a Filippi - who was paying for his previous efforts - at a speed close to fifty kilometres an hour.

Christmas came and Giulia had prepared a big tree. Fausto gave her a ring assembled with emeralds.

In the meantime, their solicitors did everything possible to convince Dr Locatelli to withdraw his action. After numerous negotiations an agreement was reached. It consisted of a sum of nine million lire being paid as damages. Locatelli further demanded that the 'White Lady' write a letter in which she accused herself in the most formal and ignominious way. It would be read to her children Lolli and Maurizo on the day of their eighteenth birthday. Finally she signed a paper renouncing all right to both of the children.

The price was heavy. Fausto wanted to oppose the signature of his companion. But he was obliged to submit for a very simple reason. She was expecting a baby and the child must carry the name of Coppi. To achieve that it must be born in a foreign country. To get there a passport was necessary. For the moment the document was withheld along with that of Fausto.

After the withdrawal of the plaint, she returned to the house at Novi. But there was still no peace. Fausto was obliged to come to an agreement with Bruna and look after the interests of his daughter, the little Marina.

This difficult settlement cost Coppi fifty million lire in property and fifty million in cash.

After the plaint was withdrawn, the accusation of abandoning the conjugal home did not cost so much.

At the end of a brief trial, they were inevitably condemned: Giulia was condemned to three months in prison, and Coppi to two months, both sentences were suspended.

When their passports were returned to them, they began to wonder in which country their child should be born. Fausto sought advice, finally everything was clear. He murmured to his companion:

'You'll have to go a long way away and perhaps for some time as well. You'll have to go Argentina.'

Fausto wanted to go with her but the Tour of Italy was starting a few days later. So she left the peninsula accompanied by Mre Lucia di Grandi, the wife of Pinella, Fausto's faithful mechanic. In all the drawers of the house she left a message: 'I love you, do not forget me.'

For the champion, the cycling season of 1955 had started and for him it seemed like all the other seasons. He won the first event on the calendar: the Circuit of Cagliari; then, at the Tour de Campania, he dominated the race, just as he had in his finest days, behind the second place man Mangi more than five minutes behind.

'It is not a victory but a triumph' could be read in the 'Gazetto dello Sport.'

In Paris-Roubaix, while the Frenchman Jean Forestier went away alone for a fine win, Coppi found himself in company with Bobet, Koblet and Van Steenbergen. He beat them at the finish and carried off second place.

He was on form for the Tour of Italy. In Cannes at the end of the second stage, he was second, beaten in the sprint by Magni.

But his thoughts were in Buenos-Aires where his companion was awaiting the birth of the Coppi child. In order to alleviate the waiting she spent several hours a day writing long letters to Fausto. After she had put them in the afternoon post, she sent him a telegram. Finally she called him on the telephone. They said practically nothing to each other; no sooner had she heard his voice than she burst into tears.

On the 13th May 1955, the child came into the world. It was a boy just like Fausto wanted. He was registered with the authorities at Buenos-Aires under the name of Coppi Angelo-Fausto-Maurizio. From the clinic she addressed the following cable to Fausto:

'Papa, I am waiting for the first pink jersey - Fausto.'

The next day she called him on the telephone waiting to hear the voice of their little son that she was holding in her arms. But the baby emitted no sound so she was obliged to shake him.

On the stage at Venice, in the Tour of Italy, Fausto received a photo of his son, a dozen kilometres after the start, he called Gino Bartali who was following the race as a reporter for Italian radio:

'Gino, come and see! I've something to show you', he said to him and held out a transparent envelope.

Bartali saw the picture of a fine baby.

Coppi was visibly happy, his pedalling became lighter, he smiled.

'I'm going to show it to everyone', said the old champion.

And the arch ex-rival of the Campionissimo spread it around the following caravan by crying out:

'Look, It's Faustino. Fausto's son!'

Everybody was happy. For several kilometres nobody thought of

Ship attendants about to help the 'White lady' leave the 'Jacques Cesar' in Cannes

attacking. It was a truce.

Unfortunately, intolerance again emerged. When the Giro passed under the Pope's window at Castelgandolfo, he refused to give the peloton his blessing. Coppi, the adulterer, an outlaw as far as the Church was concerned, was not one of the flock. A black sheep had slipped in among the good shepherds.

Coppi did not win this Tour of Italy. He nevertheless finished second, only thirteen seconds behind the winner Magni, winning the penultimate stage Trento-San Pellegrino.

The Italian passenger liner 'Julius Caeser', at the beginning of the month of June, brought Giulia and the little Fausto back to Europe. From now on the child would be known as Faustino. When the ship put in at Cannes, she got off carrying the baby in a straw basket. She would have preferred to remain anonymous but on board, the news spread like wildfire. When she came down the gangway of the boat, all the passengers were watching her from the decks or the portholes. She had to take refuge in the pilot's cabin in order to escape the photographers.

She quickly managed to reach the heights above Rocheville where she had rented a villa. Fausto came to join her there.

He kissed her without being able to say a word; no doubt being overcome with the emotion of the moment. Then he took the child in his arms, laid him on a bed and knelt down to look at him and admire him, as if nothing else existed for him.

From then on his face was lit up with pride. On his bicycle he found a second youth; being triumphant in the month of September at the Tour of the Apennines then at the Three Valleys Varesines. The victories and places of honour were achieved at the age of thirty seven - a considerable exploit.

Finally, to end the season on a high note, he carried off, for the third time, the Baracchi Trophy, partnered as usual with Ricardo Filippi.

When Christmas arrived, Faustino received presents from all corners of Europe and, naturally, his very first bicycle.

However, the shadow of the law continued to darken the happiness of the two people and even extended to their child. The son of Fausto, Faustino carried, in Argentina where he was born, his real surname: Coppi. As an Italian citizen the law required him to carry the name of his 'presumed father': Locatelli.

Enrico Locatelli would have had to present himself to a tribunal, in the required time to disavow his paternity. He had promised to do this but had not kept to his word.

Giulia and Fausto were however, ready to do everything to ensure that Faustino had the right to use the name of his father.

They had their house, they had a son; their life was the same as so

The 'White Lady' being helped at the boarding bay in Cannes on her return from Argentina with baby boy 'Faustino'

The 'White lady' and 'Faustino' in the hills above Cannes, June 1955

many other families. They had everything in the world that they could hope for. They loved each other, their boy was in good health and grew bigger. The future, even after so many painful tests, so many humiliations and so much bitterness aimed at them could at last promise some happiness.

Solitude

At thirty seven years old, Coppi was still one of the best riders of his country and always remained the captain and the soul of the Bianchi team.

For the start of the season, he chose the charming village of Cogoletto on the gulf of Genoa, just a few kilometres from the Turchino.

One morning, he returned from training and complained of being tired and feverish. At the University clinic at Genoa, typhus was diagnosed. The season was compromised. He was bitter. Once again fate had struck him down but contrary to what might had been thought, the cause of his bitterness lay elsewhere. In fact ingratitude played a part. As he could not race, the directors of Bianchi took the decision to cancel his contract with the firm.

A moral spring broke inside of him. Bianchi! The team of which he had been so proud of all his career. This sky-blue jersey whose colours he had defended for practically all of his professional career, from now on he would wear them no more. What could he do?

As usual he got over this hard blow and as soon as he was better, he assembled his own team under the patronage of the sponsor 'Carpano'. The 'Carpano-Coppi' team was born, bringing together most of his former companions who had agreed to follow him. Unfortunately misfortune returned. Another attack of typhus nailed him to his bed with a temperature of 40C on the day before the Tour of Campania.

And that was not the end of it. In the Tour of Italy on the Mantua-Rimi stage he was thrown to the ground by a crash, in company with four other riders. The diagnosis was: a sprained ankle and displaced vertebrae. He was obliged to wear an orthopaedic corset and rest for two months.

He returned to win the Grand Prix of Lugano time trial where he beat the elegant young Swiss Rolf Graf.

The crown literally exploded and on all sides hastily written banners appeared: 'Fausto, you are still the King', 'Homage to Fausto, the jet

Coppi lead's Bobet in the Tour of Lombardy, 1956

Adriaenssens (centre) and Debruyne, team members of 'Carpano-Coppi' play with little Faustino, watched over by the master

The finish of the 1956 Tour of Lombardy. André Darrigade beats the Campionissimo at the line

plane'.

The man in question was moved close to tears and said:

'At last. After all my misfortunes, great joy. I needed this victory; it had come at the right time.'

Now he turned his attention to the Tour of Lombardy. He felt in remarkable physical form.

During the course of the event, in order to test his capabilities, he launched a violent attack on the steep climb of the Madonna del Ghisallo. All his adversaries were dropped, transfixed by such an offensive, all except one, a tough roadman who he knew well: Diego Ronchini, his former team-mate who had stayed faithful to the Bianchi colours. Back in the bunch there were three other talented 'Bianchi's' like the Frenchmen Jacques Anquetil and Andre Darrigarde, taken on by the Italian team the previous year at Coppi's request, to ride events in Italy. Darrigarde had been retained, due to his talent as a sprinter. He was equal to the rapid man from Piedmont Nino Defillipis. Coppi of course regretted it now, for it meant he was up against an extra adversary in 1956.

Once the Ghisallo was climbed, a counter attack formed behind. A group grew closer to the two escapees. Among them was Andre Darrigarde. Pinalla di Grandi, the ex-mechanic and confidante of Coppi, now team manager of Bianchi, then took the decision of going to tell Ronchini not to work anymore with Coppi as his team mate Darrigarde was coming up from behind. Ronchini complied. Coppi continued, doing all the work himself but knew that it was suicidal. In fact it was only at the entrance to Milan that the former World champion was joined by a group which comprised: Andre Darrigarde, Rik Van Looy, Fred Debruyne, Miguel Poblet, Fiorenzo Magni and Louison Bobet...mostly all sprinters against whom a declining Coppi had little chance. However the Campionissimo was not ready to throw in the towel.

On the Vigorelli track at Milan, he attacked five hundred metres from the line, putting everyone in the wind and, two metres from the white line the crowd was on its feet proclaiming Coppi as the winner; but suddenly Darrigarde surged up from the eight position and with one last kick managed to get his wheel in front: first Darrigarde, second Coppi.

On the grass, the Italian champion cried bitter tears. Close to him Pinella di Grandi tried to hide his sadness as well. In fact, it was he who condemned him to defeat by ordering Ronchini to stop working in the break.

'The decision cost me a lot', sighed Pinella '...and I am devastated. I am tied to Coppi by a deep friendship and I esteem him as a man and as a rider. I know that today he fired his last cartridges, but he has

*Coppi and Bobet. A crash, 1st March at Sassari, saw Coppi
fracture a tendon in his left thigh*

Coppi convalescing with his 'family' during the Tour of Italy 1957

Coppi with Ercole Baldini winning the Baracchi Trophy 1957

become an adversary. I had to put my sentiments to one side and support Darrigarde.'

In the Trophy Baracchi a few days later, the same end was reserved for Fausto, riding again with Ricardo Filippi. Darrigarde, who had Roll Graf as a team-mate, won again. The next day the 'Gazetto dello Sport' spread its main title over five columns: 'The destiny of Coppi is called Darrigarde!'

The 1956 season was over. Did this apply to the champion's career as well? Everyone secretly thought so, except for the man himself that is, who incorrigibly did not consider it so.

In 1957, unfortunately, once again, cruel destiny stepped in. In the month of February during the races in Sardinia, he was the victim of a crash resulting in a fractured femur. Five long months of convalescence and physiotherapy were needed. Would he at last hang up his wheels? No! At the end of the season he accepted the offer of the industrialist Mino Barrachi, to ride the Trophy which carried his name, associated with the rising star of Italian cycling, Ercole Baldini, former Olympic champion and holder of the hour record.

On the 4th November the two men started the event. The race was uneventful. Fausto suffered like a martyr when his team mate went to the front. This Baldini was a real locomotive! Ercole surpassed himself. Coppi finished in agony with very little strength left, and the victory was achieved at nearly forty seven kilometres an hour. It was Coppi's last win. He was just thirty eight...

His last victory, certainly, but not his last race, as one would see.

In the month of March 1958 he rode the Paris-Nice, contested over several stages. After the fifty kilometres of the time trial stage run between Uzes and Anquetil, he finished in fourteenth place, almost five minutes down on Jacques Anquetil, who realised the fabulous average speed of nearly forty eight kilometres an hour. For Coppi it was not too bad but he was not in his usual place.

Just for the pleasure of it, he wanted to line up for one last time at the start of the Tour of Italy. Bianchi, the team of his days of glory, repented and opened their arms to him. Fausto possessed the soul of a beginner, however, he was only playing the walk-on part of an extra. At Viareggio in the stage against the watch, he finished twentieth, more than six minutes slower than Baldini.

Something very hard to bear took place in the course of this Tour of Italy, during stage six from Mondovi to Chiarivi.

The stretched out bunch was riding very quickly up a small hill. Nobody jibed at doing his turn. Suddenly a raucous cry was heard, a cry which was both an order and a supplication:

'Rallentare! Rallentare per favore!' (Slow down! Slow down please!)

And everyone discovered with amazement that it came from Fausto

Coppi, hunched over the frame of his bike with a round back and his face twisted with suffering.

'Five years ago, nobody would have dared to attack' replied a furious Fausto.

On Thursday, 28th May 1958 on a little hill that did not even count for the King of the Mountains prize, his weakness was evident to all: 'The Insuperable!', 'The Insurmountable' Fausto Coppi had finally asked for mercy.

He thought he could still serve the cycling cause. Why not become a good team man? He did not know when to stop. His sworn aim: to be included in the Italian team in the World Championships at Rheims in France. To this end he started the prestigious Three Valleys Varesines race. Alfredo Binda, the selector was there. During the course of this event, he had to designate the men who would make the journey to the City of Champagne. Fausto fought, dug deep into his reserves and finished seventh. He was recompensed for his efforts; Coppi, who was pushing thirty nine, was selected for the World Championships.

He put all his know-how at the service of the Italian formation, all his science, all his tactical sense and actively contributed to the success of his former team mate of one day: Ercole Baldini.

But he did not want to stop. He never forgot that cycling had allowed him to escape, he and his family, from poverty, almost from misery. So he continued to dedicate a sort of adoration to it.

The road became longer and the breathing more husky. However, the old athlete wanted to hear nothing of Giulia's exhortations. He behaved like a poor devil who raced because he needed the money. The people applauded him out of charity, remembering that he had been the 'greatest'. They were no longer interested in him.

'We too, wrote the journalist Bruno Raschi, we were in doubt, up until this day of April 1959 when we took our courage in our hands to go and ask him the reason for this sporting survival. We had on that day, left together to reach the place where Paris-Roubaix started, an inhuman race for an athlete of forty years who seemed to be dragging behind his fragile bicycle the heavy array of his trophies. Coppi with his past glory, should never have had to figure amongst the ranks of the martyrs. On that particular morning, between the clouds and the noise of the car engines, we had a conversation which got to the bottom of things. We looked our friend in the face and posed the question to him:

Between you and me Fausto, why do you want to go on?'

He looked at us with sad surprise, almost astonished at the question and contented himself with replying:

'Come tomorrow, to the finish of Paris-Roubaix.'

The next day he arrived, his face blackened, caked in mud but in the middle of which his eyes shone like fire and seemed to say:

'You have seen? I have done this classic again! I still have a voice,
why do you want to stop me singing?'

Coppi at home convalescing following a fall in the Tour of Sardinia 1958

THE BROKEN MAN

1959 WAS COPPI'S FORTIETH YEAR. It was way past the time for him to retire. But he did not think so. His enthusiasm remained intact. On the other hand his strength was fast diminishing. On his bike he was but a shadow of his former self.

From the beginning of the month of March, he lined up for the start of the Tour of Levant at the head of his new formation 'Tricofilina - Coppi' which had in its ranks the Spaniard Federico Bahamontes and Michele Gismondi.

On the second stage, unfortunately, he was the victim of a crash on a road under repair. With injuries to his left shoulder and arm, he was obliged to retire from the race. After a medical examination he was found to have two broken fingers.

He had scarcely returned home when fate struck again, this time during training. Ettore Milano, perched on a small motorbike was pacing him. On a road in the suburbs of Alessandria, at the end of an area known as Spinetta Marengo, a tractor came slowly out of track. Milano as normal moved to the left but Coppi behind him had not seen this sharp turn and ran straight into the tractor. he fell on the asphalt and passed out.

Knowing how fragile Fausto's bones were, Milano took fright, stopped a car and took his team leader quickly to the hospital at Alessandria. There then took place a grotesque argument between the doctors, for Coppi instead of being taken to the orthopaedic department was wheeled to the surgical wing. The orthopaedists believing that if it was Coppi, then he must have broken something. The illustrious champion had done no such thing. He was merely suffering from bruises and a lacerated scalp at the top of his forehead.

The quarrel about the competence of a doctor in front of a patient who was less injured than they believed, made certain people smile who saw that the occasion must have some publicity value. Each of these men of science, in fact, hoped that the radio, the television and at least a hundred reporters and photographers would urgently be sent to

At the start of the Tour of Spain, Coppi with Raymond Kopa,
a soccer star with Real Madrid

Alessandria to inform the cycling world about the 'latest accident which had happened to the Campionissimo'.

As soon as he was back on his feet, the hard-wearing Fausto took to his bike to ride Paris-Roubaix where he finished...in forty ninth place.

So after so many years having demonstrated an outrageous domination over his adversaries, after having won everything, after having reached the limit of the sporting deed, he is today, according to the words of a Parisian journalist Pierre Chany 'a magnificent and grotesque washout, a weary and disillusioned man, ironical towards himself, nothing except the warmth of simple friendship can penetrate his melancholia.'

He continued on his path to sporting succeed by competing in the Tour of Spain.

He covered several stages, always at the back of the peloton. He hung on, suffered like a martyr, was dropped like some anonymous also-ran. He refound his old masseur Biagio Cavanna who helped him in his 'agony'. Giulia begged him to come back home; he did not listen.

'I am eating well, he confided, I am sleeping well but I have no more strength - especially in the legs - and I do not have the will.'

On the fourteenth stage from Eibar to Vittoria, he touched rock bottom. On the Uruiola mountain he was totally exhausted. For several days people had been trying to persuade him to retire.

The next day he did not start. In his seedy hotel room, Raphael Geminiani came to see him:

'You just think 'Gem', what I have to accept ? Look, I'm stopping, I can't do this anymore'

He had nothing left. In the races he was no longer in a state to maintain the speed of the others.

In one of the races whose name has been forgotten, a very minor race which was hardly worthy of the Great Coppi, he found himself in the middle of a break which looked like being the decisive one. Fausto demonstrated an inordinate desire to once again experience the exhilaration of victory, even if it was only in a modest Criterium. His adversaries agreed to let him triumph but unfortunately when the finishing banner was almost in sight, he was the victim of a puncture and victory escaped him.

He could not surmount his fatal destiny.

And he still pursued his senseless attempt at cycling survival. On the 25th October, he was fourth in the Grand Prix of Lugano, held against the watch. On the 4th November, in the Baracchi Trophy, the organisers brought together two former aces in decline: Coppi and Bobet. They finished 5th...

And the season came to a close.

Coppi leaves on his final journey,
December 1959

In Africa, one of the last ever photos of the
'Campionissimo', relaxing with friends and
family. On the right Raphael Géminiani.

In December, Coppi accepted an invitation to go to Haute-Volta in order to participate in a small race, followed by a safari.

The trip had been arranged by Raphael Geminiani. Besides 'Gem', the expedition included five other riders: Jacques Anquetil, Roger Riviere, Roger Hassenforder, Henry Anglade and Fausto Coppi.

Fausto, the only foreigner on the journey, accepted, delighted to make the trip to Africa and particularly happy to participate in several big game hunting parties of which he was so fond.

The wives were invited but Fausto did not take Giulia. She refused and did not want him to go either

'I was fearful' she said 'I thought that it was the worst season, with extreme changes in temperature and of the illnesses that could be caught more easily in Africa than elsewhere. I said all this to him but he would not change his mind.

As the day approached , my fears became worse, I was obsessed with the idea of malaria. I had read, I had heard stories of people exhausted and brought down by the illness, stories of fever and terrible struggles in the face of death.

I saw him off from the station at Turin. Right up until the last moment I begged him to change his mind: "Fausto" I said to him "why are you leaving us all alone? Why are you going? Fausto, think, there's malaria down there..."'

But Fausto remained deaf to her supplications. He reached Paris where he had to join the other members of the expedition, the departure for Ougadougou being fixed for the 10th December.

The incorrigible Geminiani was late for the rendezvous at Ouly airport. The aeroplane was about to take off when he arrived. He explained that he had been invited to lunch by the journalist Rene de Latour who had also invited a young man whose passion was cycling, called Alain Delon. The latter was also late meaning that lunch was delayed...

After an excellent overnight journey, the plane put down at Ougadougou. They were all struck by the tropical heat.

They received an admirable welcome. Their hosts could not do enough to make their stay as agreeable as possible.

Anquetil won the seventy kilometre race in a sprint finish, in front of Coppi. Twenty thousand enthusiastic spectators were present. It was a total success. On the posters Fausto was presented as the greatest rider of all time. The local riders who pedalled in his wake and who had such names as: Sanou, Moussa, Sibiri, Kouakou and Kouame looked at him incredulously. They had never dreamed of racing against Fausto Coppi.

'We hunted partridges' Geminiani recounted 'Fausto hardly went out, he felt tired. Once, however, he did go lion hunting. After which he confessed to me: "I saw a lioness with its cubs, but I didn't shoot, the sight of them was too beautiful."'

Another important witness appeared, Maurice Maurel, at the time a reporter for L'Equipe and the only journalist on the expedition.

'I arrived at Ouagodougou on Sunday 13th December' wrote the journalist 'I came from Abidjan where I received a 'phone call telling me to go the capital of Haute-Volta...When I disembarked at Ouagodougou, the night had fallen and the criterium had long since finished. I went in search of the riders. Fortunately there was no light in the sky and the streets were dark and after several kilometres in a rattly taxi, the illuminated garden of a villa caught my attention. That was certainly the place. It was a reception organised in honour of the riders.

The evening continued with a dance given in honour of cycling, in the hangar of the aero-club, attended by various African VIP's and presided over by Mr Maurice Yameogo, president of the Republic of Haute-Volta, democratically seated on a garden chair.

The president put at the disposition of the champions, the two 'Broussard' aeroplanes of the republican presidency, so that they could go on safari. This was on the 14th December. In fact it consisted of a hunting party organised by volunteer guides, among whom were the organisers of the criterium, who had spontaneously put themselves at the disposition of the patrol. Those who were unable to find a place in the aircraft went by car to Fada N'Gourma, situated about one hundred and fifty kilometres from the capital which constituted the last port of call before the reserve of Borga, a hunter's paradise. It was also where the team would be staying.

In the evening, Coppi and Geminiani were put up in the magnificent villa of a certain Bonanza, the head of a large construction company, who was delighted to have Coppi in his home. He invited everybody to a huge reception to meet the archbishop and the Chief of Police.

Maurice Maurel wrote in his notebook: 'the evening is lively and gay; it was only Coppi who did not really join in.'

Geminiani managed to cheer him up. He embraced him, visibly happy, and said to him:

'At least Gem, we've found each other!'

'Then we were stretched out on our beds, in the same room. As usual we found ourselves under attack from the mosquitoes. After several slaps, I went to sleep exhausted. He continued to fight all night long. The next day he was very tired.'

The following day, Fausto left for the hunt and only saw the other Frenchman once, around a roast boar killed by Roger Riviere.

After he had been presented to the president of the Republic of Haute-Volta, Maurice Maurel noted again, Coppi replied easily in French with hardly any accent. That evening he was stooped with weariness. Bags had formed under his eyes. He was a pale colour in spite of the burning sun. He had difficulty in stifling his yawns and no doubt wished it was all over.'

All the members of the expedition took a last meal together on Thursday, 17th December at Abidjan airport from where they were leaving. Fausto still appeared very tired. He expressed the intention of getting back to Italy as quickly as possible. He achieved this, in company with his friend Cillerio, vice president of the Turin Football Club and Raphael Geminiani, by finding three seats on the plane leaving for Paris, while the others after a last reception at the Bar des Sports, did not take off until the following day.

Coppi then took the plane from Paris to Turin. Giulia, to whom he had spoken on the 'phone, had arranged to meet him at the airport. Unfortunately, due to the fog, the plane was diverted to Milan-Malpensa. Fausto succeeded in reaching her on the telephone.

So Giulia wanted to get back to the villa first to greet him. She drove back madly through the fog. She won this test of speed but when Fausto arrived, she cried out:

'Oh! You look terrible.'

His face made a big impression on her. It appeared yellow and wrinkled. His clothes were crumpled and his hair disarranged.

'It's nothing' he said, and turned towards Faustino who jumped into his arms. 'The race was interesting', he added to his companion, 'but the hunting and the country was a disaster. They would have to pay me a lot to go back again!'

As on each journey, Fausto returned with a lot of presents for his son. This time he had chosen some model aeroplanes.

'When he had washed', Giulia wrote later, 'Fausto looked a lot better to me. He had recovered his energy and was happy. Everything seemed normal. The next day we went shooting and the day after we went to Genoa for a football match in which Genoa was playing Alessandria, a great Piedmont derby.'

The daily life went by once again, calmly and peacefully. Fausto visited his hunting reserve at Incise Scapacino, then on the 23rd December went to Milan for an event.

Christmas Eve arrived. Each year the same ritual was repeated. After the appearance of Father Christmas, Fausto and Giulia released some hydrogen balloons carrying a message from Faustino to the infant Jesus. The balloons disappeared into the grey sky. Then Father Christmas arrived, announced by a great ringing of bells and a rain of little chocolates. Towards eleven o'clock Coppi went down into the cellar for some bottles of champagne.

'On that particular evening', Giulia recounted, 'I was seized with a strange melancholy. I wanted to do nothing. It seemed as if I no longer wanted to take part in the festivities.

Christmas Day seemed just like all the previous ones had been. We had several members of the family to lunch. The sadness of the previous evening had not left me. When we came to sit down to lunch, Fausto noted that I had not changed.

"Why haven't you dressed?" he asked me

"I feel very sad", I replied, "I don't know why."

Fausto was calm and relaxed.'

Coppi's famous masseur Cavanna gives the champion some expert attention in front of a captive audience

THE CAMPIONISSIMO IS NO MORE.

ON THE 26TH DECEMBER, Fausto, Giulia and Faustino went for a drive to Nice. It was a beautiful day. A radiant Fausto announced to his companion that he was going to race for one more year. She did not argue with him. On that subject he remained the master.

Faustino ran and jumped around like children of his age did. He told his parents that he would no longer be a singer when he grew up.

The next day the former World Champion went to his hunting reserve in a dense fog. No break in the weather was expected.

He came back at about one o'clock in the afternoon very tired, with a waxy complexion.

'It seems to me', he confided, ' as if I have a fever. At one time I though I was going to pass out at the steering wheel. I'm sorry but you will have to have lunch without me.'

He went up to his room and went to bed. Giulia helped him to undress and called the doctor, Dr Allegri. Half and hour later he arrived at the bedside of the sick man.

His visit was a quick one.

'It's 'flu' he said 'Just flu.'

'You don't think it's malaria?' asked Giulia

'Malaria? Certainly not.' he replied.

Fausto's condition very quickly worsened. In the evening he was seized with a violent fit of vomiting. Consulted again, Dr Allegri prescribed injections which had a base of solucamphor. The vomiting still continued then Fausto, exhausted, went to sleep.

Dr Allegri came twice the following day but did not change the treatment. The sick man was thirsty, very thirsty. He was given mineral water and fresh orange juice. Giulia did the best she could for him.

On Tuesday 29th December, she took the decision to telephone Professor Giovanni Astaldi who knew the family well. The professor stayed a long time with Fausto, but he too diagnosed nothing more than 'flu.

'It's a type of 'flu that has been laying people low this year,' he added.

'The symptoms are clear.'

Downstairs he signed a prescription including a urine test but no blood test.

He too shook his head when malaria was mentioned.

On the 30th December the patient's condition was stable. He was still tormented by thirst. Professor Astaldi and Dr Allegri came back to see him. The latter seemed rather optimistic:

'There is no more risk at the moment,' he said, 'But we did fear an inflammation of the liver...'

Giulia continued to sit up with him the following night. His condition seemed to improve. The vomiting stopped, Fausto managed to get a little food down and the fever seemed better.

The last day of the year arrived. Angiolina, Fausto's mother was expected with Uncle Giuseppe and several friends who were coming to present their wishes for the new year. They came; then Fausto and Giulia found themselves alone again. At midnight the patient had to have another injection. But even before the clock stuck twelve, he started to toss around. He was again tortured with thirst. Sweat ran down his face and he did not stop complaining.

'I spent hours and hours', Giulia recounted, 'moistening his face with a flannel filled with crushed ice, moistening his lips with orange and lemon juice. I took his temperature. I quickly phoned Dr Allegri who told me to give him an injection to stimulate the heart. For a moment I thought that Fausto was no longer breathing but after the injection an improvement was seen and he started to doze. The sleep did not last long. Fausto started to pant; his great chest rose and fell at an ever increasing rate. That was the way the night passed.

In the morning; New Year's Day 1960, Dr Allegri arrived, examined Fausto and wanted to immediately consult with Professor Astaldi. We also called Professor Aminta Fieschi, the director of the Institute of Pathology of Special Medicine at the University of Genoa.

Fausto was getting worse all the time. I saw one hand on his chest and the other arm extended. The long consultation finally came to nothing - according to the words of the doctors - a still uncertain diagnosis. Fausto would have to be taken to the clinic. I asked him why.

'Take the decision' he said to me.

I resolved to obey the doctors and gave permission for him to be transported to hospital. But where? To Pavia? to Tortona? Waiting for the ambulance to arrive, it was decided to drive him to Tortona. This hospital was directed by Professor Astaldi. In this way Coppi would have by his side the doctor who had followed him since the beginning of his illness.

The ambulance arrived and the nurse went upstairs with the stretcher. Fausto had never wanted his son to see him stretched out on one of these sad little beds. On that day however, he asked to see Faustino.

Coming out of the bedroom, the nurses put the stretcher on the floor
'Come back soon, Papa' said Faustino
'Yes, my treasure. Good-bye and be good.'

As they brought him out of the house, Fausto continued to make signs with his hands. He still hesitated over the choice of hospitals. Pavia or Tortona? In the ambulance Fausto declared that it was all the same to him, and we stopped at Tortona.'

It was then learned that in France, at Clermont-Ferrand, Raphael Geminiani found himself bedridden with the same symptoms as Fausto. On the day after Christmas, the 'big gun' - as he was familiarly known - had to leave the table as he appeared to be exhausted. Those who knew of the outrageous health of Geminiani, could measure just how hard the illness had struck him.

He collapsed as if he had been electrified. His tongue was lively and his hair came out in handfuls.

'I told my wife', Raphael said, 'I really believe I've got malaria. It was more by intuition than by medical knowledge. Later I learned that it was known as 'Plasmodium Falciparum', a fatal malaria parasite.'

For three days Dr Mora, the physician in charge, treated him for a violent crisis of hepatitis, jaundice and a thyroid gland. It achieved nothing. The illness got worse. The temperature of the patient went up to 41.6 degrees. He was coming close to death.

The doctor then administered a strong dose of phenergan to knock him out as he was becoming delirious. Before that he had been given x-rays and other examinations.

Fortunately, at the time there happened to be a certain Dr Brugiere passing through Clermont-Ferrand, who was a specialist in tropical medicine. He concluded that the malady was due to a parasite present in the body.

A sample of blood was hastily despatched to Paris and the Pasteur Institute where Professor Schneidner's diagnosis was a case of malaria of which the parasite attacked the red globules in the blood and destroyed them in eight days.

Raphael Geminiani was saved in extremis.

'I fought as hard as I could against this accursed illness,' he said later, 'Each day which passed was different to the one before. I quickly went from comatose periods to one of lucidity. At this time I was obliged to summon enormous willpower to pull me through. I fear for Coppi in his comatose condition.'

When the exact nature of the illness was verified, Geminiani's brother Angelo, telephoned Novi Ligure to try to speak to the doctor who was treating Fausto and to make him aware of the diagnosis from the Pasteur Institute. The doctor replied: 'Let them treat your brother for what he is suffering from, we will treat Coppi as we think fit.'

When Coppi arrived at the hospital at Tortona, he was taken straight to radiography. The great champion was suffering a lot. They had to move his position several times to take the x-rays. But when everything was ready, the machine broke down and the pictures were not taken.

During this time, on the evening of the 1st January 1960, all departments were put on a state of alert.

Were they going to find out - finally - the nature of the illness? Very quickly a diagnosis was put forward that Professor Astaldi had always insisted on: viral bronchial-pneumonia.

Night fell on the hospital and Fausto became weaker while the professors and doctors questioned each other over the course of treatment to follow. They opted for cortisone and antibiotics. A tragic error. Not only would the cortisone have no power to heal but it would also have the reverse effect to the one required.

He was given cortisone up until one o'clock in the morning. They believed they detected an improvement in the patient's condition. It seems it was what is commonly known as 'the best of the end'.

From then on the worst was feared. Olimpia, Uncle Fausto's wife called Bruna Ciampolini, the eternal legitimate wife of Coppi, to the hospital. Ettore Milano and Livio brought her in by one door while Giulia came in through another entrance so the women did not come face to face.

Fausto saw Bruna. According to Professor Astaldi he closed his eyes and covered his face with his hand. No sound escaped from his lips.

Let us leave the 'white lady' to recount the last moments of the Campionissimo:

'Uncle Guiseppe came to find me in the chapel and said to me:

"Madame Giulia, Fausto is dying. What is your position? What is to be done?"

"I only want Fausto not to be aware that he is going to die" I replied.

The last hours of Fausto were as long as eternity. About three o'clock in the morning, Professor Fiechi declared:

"If he gets through the night, there is still hope."

At half past three the hospital chaplain gave him extreme unction. It was said that Fausto had confessed. This is untrue. Before the priest arrived, I tried to see his tongue. With great difficulty he opened his mouth, he understood me and he heard me but he could not move his tongue. I touched it with a finger: it was all furrowed, as if it was burnt. Fausto was no longer, physically, able to talk. The fever had risen above 40 degrees, the pulse was one hundred and eighty,

He did not reply when the priest offered to hear his confession.

While the drama was being played out, the dawn started to appear through the window. A damp overcast day. Fausto was breathing with difficulty. I was broken up listening to him. He emitted six groans and then suddenly the breathing stopped.'

It was 8:45 am, Saturday 2nd January 1960.

Ettore Milano, in a state of collapse, eventually was able to go to Coppi's villa to collect his clothes. He chose a grey suit with stripes brought a short time before in Turin. It suited Fausto so well that his friends enjoyed saying to him:

'Fausto, you look like a real Parisian in that.'

Fausto, 'the Prince of Elegance' returned to the house of his birth to the sound of the bells who were crying for his errant son who had come back to his hills forever.

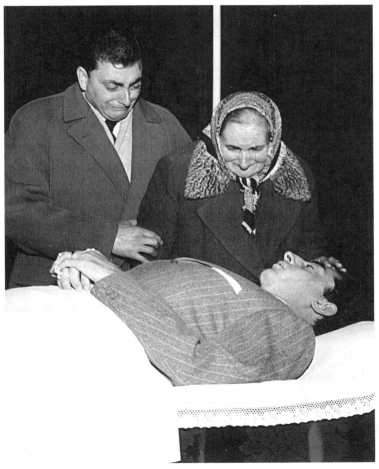

A heartbroken family. 'Mamma' Coppi and brother Livio before the Campionissimo is put to rest

Notices stuck up announcing the death of Fausto Coppi. (With the wrong date)

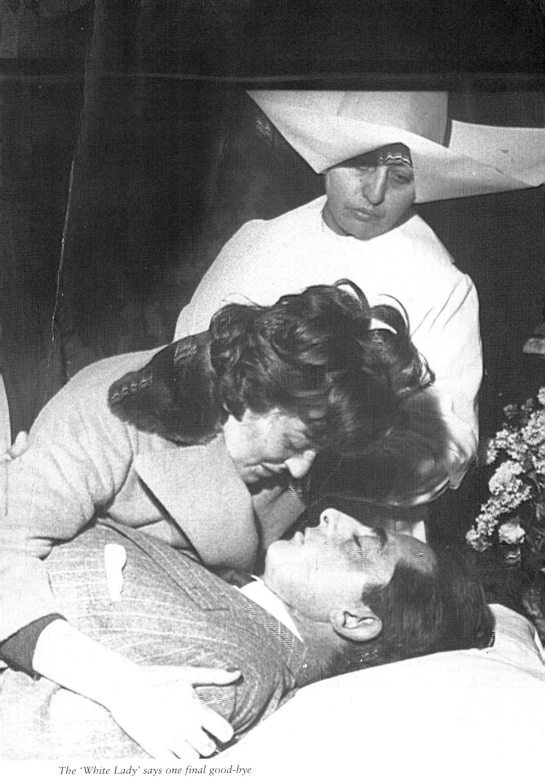

The 'White Lady' says one final good-bye

The funeral of the 'Campionissimo'. 4th January 1960

A NATION CRIES

BEFORE THE FUNERAL OF THE GREAT CHAMPION, an immense crowd went to the chapel of rest, then assembled on the road used by the funeral cortege to reach Castellania. Among the witnesses was Jean Bobet who wrote in the newspaper 'L'Equipe':

'For the last time the crowd pressed towards him. No, not the noisy hysterical crowd of the 'tifosi' who acclaimed Fausto, as the Milan-San Remo passed through, or everywhere else in cycling events the world over. But a contemplative and silent crowd, peasants who came down from all the valleys, tourists surprised by the awful news, sportsmen close to collapse, friends who had hurried from all over the country. Since noon on Saturday, this crowd had filed past the mortal remains of the greatest champion ever known. This sad crowd who had come to pay their last respects to a hero who from now on would have to be spoken of in the past tense...It was yesterday at three o'clock that Fausto was brought to the house of his birth at Castellania, then to the village cemetery. It was impossible to imagine that this was the last journey of the great champion. Hundreds of cars accompanied the hearse over the last twenty kilometres of the route, I saw the peasants on their doorsteps to salute for one last time their illustrious compatriot...At the time that these lines are being written, hundreds and hundreds of people continue to file past in the muddy road from Castellania where the 'mama' of Fausto is conducting herself with extraordinary dignity.'

The date of the funeral was fixed for the 4th January and it was there at the heart of his native village that Coppi received the supreme goodbye.

From daybreak, a crowd of pedestrians, car drivers and motorcyclists came together on the little bumpy road of the locality. The fog was so dense that it became impossible to distinguish the road two metres in front. Snow covered the sides. People sunk into the mud up to their ankles but nobody complained of the effort.

Over three hundred metres of wreaths of flowers were on display. Hung on the walls and coming from all corners of Italy and abroad.

There were eighty six of them and they gave the impression of travelling between two walls of flowers.

The mortuary was one of the highest buildings in the village. In the bedroom with whitewashed walls where Coppi was resting, a photo of his brother Serse could be seen.

People cried hot tears before the coffin. Had Coppi not been the greatest of champions and the simplest of men, a man with a generous heart who received with closed eyes the recognition of the sporting world. A paralytic to whom he had once given ten thousand lire had become healed and had walked the road to Piedmont to say his last goodbye.

One could never say how many people were there, perched on the snowy embankments, who were waiting for the passage of Coppi, on the road of his last stage.

When the cortege formed up at ten o'clock, it was preceded by two men carrying a portrait of the champion in his rainbow jersey. Pious hands had surrounded it with a thousand flowers; then the interminable column of wreath-carriers. The choristers surrounded the coffin carried by old companions of Fausto: Milano, Carrea, Pezzi, Magni, De Filipis, Conterno, Piazza, Baffi, Baldini and Coletto.

Bartali was there looking very pale, as were Anquetil, Bobet and Darrigarde who had also come over the difficult roads to say goodbye to their highly respected rival and friend.

Suddenly, the cortege left the road and branched off towards a slope that was so steep that one could be afraid that the carriers might slip in the mud, under the weight of the coffin. Everyone climbed with difficulty, towards the picturesque church on top of the hill in San Biagio.

Some men fell. Women fainted. How would the old 'mamma' be able to reach the summit of her calvary?

The 'white lady' had spared the too young, Faustino, from enduring this sad event. She went into the church and a lot of people were astonished to see the entrance of this 'sinner' - as far as the laws of the Catholic Church were concerned - into a house of worship. It was later learned that the priest at the hospital at Tortona, Don Ferrarazzo, had been authorised to give extreme unction to Fausto Coppi - a sinner before God - on the sole condition that the 'white lady' promised the religious authorities: 'If Fausto Coppi should survive, I would let him return to his family.' In this way the Church had obtained the renunciation of the state of sin which was a prerequisite for the Church to authorise absolution. By way of consequence, Giulia too obtained absolution.

Three times she fainted in church and was eventually taken home unconscious to Nove Ligure.

'There was everything in this Italian burial,' explained Maurice Maurel, a witness to Coppi's last trip: 'an immense portrait, balanced on the end of the arm, a woman in tears, those muttering with their rosaries, crowds running across the fields to get one last view of the cortege which trailed along the serpentine road, the bustling of this same crowd to which entry to the church was forbidden, the meeting between the 'white lady' who led the cortege and Bruna who had gone directly to the presbytery to be present at the funeral service, an improbable stampede towards the cemetery, wreaths dissected, flowers and stalks taken away as souvenirs.'

Raphael Geminiani was able to be saved. Fausto Coppi was dead. The Italian press rose up. Had the great champion been properly cared for? Was he not the victim of an error of diagnosis?

The Italian newspapers launched a first offensive and on the 7th January the Provincial Sanitary Office of Alessandria made public the result of the research ordered by the Italian Minister of Health. The work, carried out by Professor Alfredo Romanzi, Director of the Institute of Microbiology at the University of Genoa, revealed that the parasites of malaria were present in Coppi's blood, just as they had been in Geminiani's.

The next day all the Italian press, picking up the accusations of the 'white lady' and relying on the analysis, agreed that Coppi should have been saved.

On the 9th January Professor Astaldi replied, saying that he and his colleagues had been confronted with extremely complex symptoms, with an organism predisposed to infectious illnesses. This was an explanation which satisfied no one as the sample of Geminiani's blood was there to demonstrate that perhaps not everything had been tried to save Coppi. It was remembered that already, in 1945, he had been victim to a first bout of paludian fever when he came back from captivity in Tunisia.

Dr Algeri, for his part, affirmed that in the beginning everything pointed to a simple illness.

'On the night of the 31st December and the 1st January,' he added 'the patient's condition rapidly deteriorated. It was only then, knowing of his journey to Africa, could symptoms of malaria be considered.'

At the very least this was disturbing as it had been known since the 19th December that Coppi had returned from Haute-Volta. Why had no blood samples been immediately analysed? Why had the anguished appeal, launched from the other side of the Alps by Angelo Geminiani, not been listened to? When it was known that, even in 1960, that malaria even in its most acute form was easily curable, one has a measure of the errors committed and one understands better the indignation of the public. For popular good sense, there was something shocking about the affair. Emotion superseded passion, the debate took on another dimension, passing from the medical domain to the more controversial one of politics. So eleven days after the death of the Campionissimo, an Italian Member of Parliament, himself a doctor, made a written request to see the Minister of Public Health and addressed the matter in these terms:

'Does the minister hold true to the habits, the seriousness and to the dignity of the profession and to the professional secret, the way of communicating the information concerning the illness and the death of Fausto Coppi, communiqués and controversies which have transformed a clinical case into a public scandal?'

The controversy, in these circumstances was without any doubt regrettable, but the public had the right to be informed, for the passing away of a man such as Fausto Coppi was not only a clinical case. The incompetent intervention and the delayed action of this deputy, who being one of the first to speak of a 'public scandal', could only reinforce the doubts about the circumstances of a death felt everywhere as one of the most painful events that sport had known for a very long time.

Was it to exonerate himself that Professor Astaldi believed it right to add: 'Coppi was very weak. His heart was afflicted by his efforts. He had already experienced a crisis two years previously. A new attack of a cardiac nature stopped Coppi from being able to resist until the time the antibiotics acted.'

Certainly, Coppi had a tired organism. The illness came to him when he was in an extremely feeble state, prematurely worn out by a long, a too long career; an attempt at sporting survival. But one remains convinced that he could still have been saved.

From now on, Coppi rests in peace.

'Death was lying in wait for him,' wrote Jacques Goddet in L'Equipe, on the day following his passing away; 'It was delighted to install him, intact, life eternal. There he will be unable to dissipate his glory, nor to submit to the affront of ageing. Let us not efface the radiant souvenirs of the victories á la Coppi. Fausto will remain installed in legend, as on a bronze pedestal.

It had been cruelly expected. But he still always wanted to be, in spite of his extreme fragility, a racing cyclist. He threw down an insane challenge to the forces of decline. He was always happy to be the most sought after, the one who was acclaimed the loudest. We would like to have cried out to him: 'Stop!' And as nobody dared to, destiny took care of it.

Fausto Coppi will race no more.'

A young Bernard Hinault visiting the Coppi memorial during the Tour of Italy 1980

Fausto Coppi Palmarés

1938 *(Amateur)*
1st   Castello d'Orba

1939 *(Independent)*
1st   Tour of Penice
1st   Pavie's Town Cup
1st   Canepa Cup
1st   Circuit of Susa
1st   Tour of Cosentino
1st   Varese's Prize
2nd Spezia-Genoa
2nd Bernocchi Cup *(PRO)*
3rd Tour of Piedmont *(PRO)*
3rd Tour of the Appennines *(PRO)*
3rd Tour of the Turin Province *(team time trial - PRO)*
3rd Tour of the Milan Province *(team time trial with Rigoni - PRO)*
6th Circuit of Savone *(PRO)*

1940 *(Professional)*
1st   Pursuit Championship of Italy
1st   Tour of Italy *(1st at Modere, 2nd at Ortisei and Genoa)*
3rd Three Valleys Varesines
3rd Grand Prix of Rome
4th Maschini Cup
5th Tour of the Milan Province *(team time trial)*
6th Road Race Championship of Italy
Equal 6th Milan-San Remo
7th Circuit of Lucca
7th Circuit of Novi-Ligure
9th Tour of Campanie
12th Tour of Piedmont
13th Circuit of Florence

13th Bernocchi Cup
16th Tour of Lombardy

1941

1st   Pursuit Championship of Italy
1st   Road Race Championship of Italy
1st   Tour of Tuscany
1st   Tour of Emile
1st   Tour of Veneto
1st   Three Valleys Varesines
1st   Tour of the Milan Province *(team time trial with Ricci)*
2nd Circuit of Rome
2nd Marin Cup at Pavie
6th   Circuit of Florence
6th   Tour of Lombardy

1942

World Hour Record
1st   Road Race Championship of Italy
1st   Pursuit Championship of Italy
2nd Tour of the Milan Province *(team time trial with De Benedetti)*
4th   Tour of Lazio
4th   Circuit of Milan
5th   Tour of Tuscany
5th   Tour of Emile
7th   Tour of Lombardy
10th Tour of Campany

1945

1st   Salvioni Cup
1st   Candelotti Cup
1st   Circuit of the As in Milan *(1st Italian race after the war)*
1st   Lugano Criterium
1st   Circuit of Ospedaletti
2nd Milan-Varzi *(1st Serse Coppi)*
2nd Circuit of Savone
2nd Tour of Lazio
3rd   Circuit of Trentino
3rd   Circuit of Genoa
3rd   Milan-Turin
5th   Italian Championship

1946

1st Milan-San Remo
1st Tour of Romagne
1st Tour of Lugano
1st Grand Prix des Nations
1st Tour of Lombardy
1st Circuit of Trocadero
2nd Tour of Italy *(1st at Bologna,Auronzo,Bassano del Grappa and Milan)*
2nd Circuit of Longchamp
2nd Championship of Zurich
3rd Circuit of Genoa
5th Circuit of Asti
6th Circuit of Bologna

1947

1st World Pursuit Championship
1st Road Race Championship of Italy
1st Tour of Italy *(1st at Prato, Naples and Trente, 2nd at Pieve and Milan, and 1st King of the Mountains)*
1st Tour of Romagne
1st Tour of Veneto
1st Tour of Emile
1st Tour of Lombardy
1st Grand Prix des Nations
1st Travers Lausanne
2nd Grand Prix Raguse
2rd Geneva Criterium
4th Circuit of Vigevano
5th Tour of Switzerland *(1st at Geneva, 2nd at Sion)*
6th Circuit of Novare
Edmond-Gentil Trophee

1948

1st Milan-San Remo
1st Tour of Emile
1st Three Valleys Varesines
1st Tour of Lombardy
2nd Circuit 'Het Volk'
2nd Road Race Championship of Italy
5th Tour of Tuscany
8th Circuit of Trevise
Retired in the Tour of Italy *(1st at Cortina d'Ampezzo and Trente and 2nd at Genoa)*
N.B. Despite retiring from Tour of Italy records show he was awarded the King of the Mountains title.

1949

1st Milan-San Remo
1st Tour of Lombardy
1st Tour of Romagne
1st Tour of Veneto
1st Tour of Italy *(1st at Salerno, Bolzano, Pinerolo, 2nd at Montecatini,*
and 1st King of the Mountains)
1st Tour of France *(1st at La Rochelle, Aoste, Nancy, 2nd at Briancon, and*
         1st King of the Mountains)
1st World Pursuit Championship
1st Road Race Championship of Italy
1st Circuit of Lauviere
2nd Tour of Piedmont
2nd Circuit of Treviglio
2nd Criterium des As *(Paris)*
3rd Fleche Wallonne
3rd Circuit of Ostie
3rd Circuit of Vimercate
4th Prato Criterium
Trophy Desgrange-Colombo Challenge

1950

1st Paris-Roubaix
1st Fleche Wallonne
1st Tour of Reggio de Calabre
1st Circuit of Genoa
2nd Rome-Naples-Rome *(1st at Latina)*
2nd Grand Prix of Lugano
2nd Baracchi Trophy *(with Serse Coppi)*
3rd Tour of Lombardy
3rd Circuit of Bordighiera
5th Tour of Piedmont
5th Grand Prix Vienna
9th Milan-San Remo

1951

1st Grand Prix Lugano
1st Grand Prix Braaschaat
1st Sables d'Olonne Criterium
2nd Tour of Romagne
2nd Grand Prix des Nations
2nd Oran Criterium
3rd Tour of Lombardy
3rd Ronde of Aix-en-Provence

Lap of honour after a magnificent victory in the 1952 Tour de France

Coppi and Van Steenbergen close to the finish in the 1952 Paris-Roubaix.
The Belgian won the sprint

4th Tour of Italy *(1st at Terni and Bolzano, 2nd at San Marino and Cortina)*

4th Criterium des As *(Paris)*

4th Baracchi Trophy *(with Van Est)*

6th Circuit of Macerata

10th Tour of France *(1st at Briancon)*

1952

1st Tour of France *(1st at Nancy, Alpe d'Huez, Sestrieres, Pau and Puy-de-Dome, 2nd at Namen)*

1st Tour of Italy *(1st at Rocca di Papa, Bozano and Como)*

1st Grand Prix Mediterranee *(1st at Foggia, Bari and Syracuse)*

1st Grand Prix Lugano

1st Tarascon Criterium

1st Auch Criterium

1st Vallorbe Criterium

2nd Paris-Roubaix

3rd Tour of Emile

3rd Baracchi Trophy *(with Gismondi)*

4th Tour of Normandy

1953

1st World Road Race Championship

1st Tour of Italy *(1st at Roccaraso, Bolzano and Bormio)*

1st Golden Bowl Monedieres *(Bol d'Monedieres)*

1st Baracchi Trophy *(with Filippi)*

1st Circuit of Borgosesia

1st Grand Prix Firminy

1st Circuit of the As at Tortona

1954

1st Tour of Lombardy

1st Bernocchi Cup

1st Tour of Campanie

1st Barrachi Trophy *(with Filippi)*

1st Circuit of Cagliari

1st St Etienne-Vergeze Stage Paris-Nice *(retired)*

2nd Italian Road Race Championship

2nd Rome-Naples-Rome *(1st at Latina and Rome)*

2nd Tour of Calabre

4th Milan-San Remo

4th Tour of Italy *(1st at Palermo T.T.T. and Bolzano)*

4th Tour of Switzerland *(1st at Davos, Lugano, 1st King of the mountains)*

6th World Road Race Championship

Lap of honour as World Champion at Lugano, 1953

1955

1st Road Race Championship of Italy
1st Tour of the Appennines
1st Three Valleys Varesines
1st Tour of Campanie
1st Baracchi Trophy *(with Filippi)*
1st Circuit of Cagliari
1st Grand Prix Van Cauthem
1st Grand Prix Titano at San Marino
2nd Tour of Italy *(1st at San Pellegrino, 2nd at Cannes, Rome and Ravenna)*
2nd Paris-Roubaix
2nd Milan-Modene
2nd Tour of Romagne
3rd Rome-Naples-Rome *(1st at Rome)*
4th Milan-Turin
5th Tour of Calabre

1956

1st Grand Prix Lugano
1st Grand Prix Campari
1st Namur Criterium
2nd Tour of Lombardy
2nd Bernocchi Cup
2nd Baracchi Trophy *(with Filippi)*
4th Golden Wheel *(with Milano)*
4th Grand Prix Asti
4th Circuit of Lavis
4th Circuit of Maria Vez
6th Circuit of San Marin
7th Road Race Championship of Italy
9th Milan-Vignola

1957

1st Baracchi Trophy *(with Baldini)*
2nd Circuit of Vigevano
3rd Circuit of Alessandria
3rd Grand Prix Lugano
3rd Nuoro Criterium
5th Circuit of Collechio

1958

1st Six days of Buenos Aires *(with Batiz)*
1st Versailles Criterium *(with Batiz)*
1st Circut of Calvisano

2nd European Criterium at Nantua
2nd Circuit of Capri
2nd Circuit of Annecy
2nd Grand Prix Cademortori
3rd Circuit of Lecoo
3rd Circuit of Valeggio
4th Circuit of Vigevano
4th Circuit of Forli
4th Circuit of Trieste
5th Circuit of San Daniele
5th Circuit of Cirie
5th Circuit of Callechio
6th Six days of Paris *(with Batiz and Plattner)*
9th Tour of Piedmont

1959
1st Grand Prix "Progres" at Lyon *(with Terruzzi)*
2nd Team Time Trial in the Tour of the Levant *(with Bahamontes and Gismondi)*
2nd Circuit of Cirie
3rd Grand Prix Verbania
3rd Circuit of Mondovi
3rd Circuit of Galiate
3rd Circuit of Gonzaga
4th Grand Prix Lugano
5th Grand Prix Forli
5th Baracchi Trophy (with Bobet)
Retired in the Tour of Spain (which was his last stage race)
after finishing 3rd in the team time trial at Retiro, and 5th in a similar stage
at San Sebastian.
On the 2nd of October, Fausto Coppi's ride at Cenon was his last race in
France.
On the 15th of December, he is 2nd in his last race, behind Anquetil:
The Ouagadougou Criterium (Haute-Volta).

Total wins 138. (Road)

His 95 Individual Pursuits

COPPI WAS AN EXCEPTIONAL RIDER on the track winning two World pursuit titles in 1947 and 1949 and the Italian Championship no less than five times in 1940, 1941, 1942, 1947 And 1948. According to records, he rode ninety-five pursuit races winning eighty-four, an outstanding record.

Coppi rode against all the other pursuit greats of his era, such as Koblet, Van Steenbergen, Bevilacqua, Kubler, Schulte, Patterson, Gillen, Magni and Bizzi beating them all at some time. However his last pursuit race was when he was past his best and was beaten by the current World pursuit champion, the great Guido Messina at Milan in October of 1995. Messina was to go on and win the title for the next two years after taking the title twice as an amateur.

1939
28-10
- at Turin: beat Magni
- at Turin: beaten by Bizzi

1940
30-6
- at Milan: beat Introzzi
- at Milan: beat Leoni
- at Milan: beat Bizzi
18-9
- at Milan: beat Bizzi
28-9
- at Milan: caught Wengler
28-10
- at Turin: beat Bizzi
17-11
- at Berlin: caught Wengler
8-12
- at Zurich: caught Kubler

1941
2-2
- at Zurich: caught Bartali
14-6
- at Milan: beat Magni
- at Milan: beat Bizzi
15-6
- at Milan: beat Saponetti
3-8
- at Milan: beat Bizzi
5-10
- at Milan: beat Bizzi
12-10
- at Milan: caught Wesenberg

1942
26-4
- at Milan: caught Kubler
24-5
- at Elberfield: caught Wesenberg

19-6
- at Milan: beat Bevilacqua
- at Milan: beat Bizzi
4-10
- at Milan: caught Cinelli

1945
23-9
- at Turin: caught Conte
- at Turin: beaten by Ortelli
- at Turin: beat Canavesi

1946
10-8
- at Milan: Ronconi
11-8
- at Milan: beat Bizzi
- at Milan: beaten by Ortelli
19-9
- at Milan: beat Peters
8-12
- at Paris: beat Pedersen
- at Paris: beat Ortelli
29-12
- at Paris: caught Blanchet

1947
5-1
- at Paris: beat Kubler
19-1
- at Saint Étienne: caught Blanchet
- at Saint Étienne: beaten by Prat
26-1
- at Paris: beat Van Steenbergen
- at Paris: beat Prat
9-2
- at Brussels: beaten by Van Steenbergen
- at Brussels: caught by Schulte
23-6
- at Milan: beat Magni
- at Milan: beat Bevilacqua
- at Milan: beat Ortelli
27-7
- at Paris: beat Lanz

29-7
- at Paris: beat Rioland
30-7
- at Paris: beat Schulte
- at Paris: beat Bevilacqua
6-9
- at Zurich: beat Koblet
29-11
- at Anvers: beat Middelkamp
- at Anvers: caught Van Steenbergen
30-11
- at Brussels: beat Impanis
- at Brussels: caught Peters
14-12
- at Ghent: caught Van Steenbergen
19-12
- at Paris: caught Blanchet

1948
4-1
- at Paris: caught Peters
- at Paris: caught Van Steenbergen
11-1
- at Ghent: beat Bevilacqua
17-1
- at Brussels: caught Middelkamp
- at Brussels: caught Blanchet
18-1
- at Nice: caught Piel
24-1
- at Anvers: beat Kaers
- at Anvers: beat Blanchet
25-1
- at Ghent: caught Blanchet
- at Ghent: caught Spelte
- at Ghent: caught Debacker
1-2
- at Brussels: beat Blanchet
- at Brussels: caught Van Steenbergen
8-2
- at Paris: beat Pedersen
- at Paris: caught Koblet
16-6
- at Rome: beat Monari

17-6
- at Rome: beat Magni
- at Rome: beat Bevilacqua

7-7
- at Milan: beat Piel
- at Milan: beat Koblet

23-8
- at Amsterdam: beat Adrianssens
- at Amsterdam: beat Gillen

24-8
- at Amsterdam: caught Bevilacqua

25-8
- at Amsterdam: beaten by Schulte

12-12
- at Paris: beat Rioland

1949
12-1
- at Paris: beat Schulte

10-4
- at Milan: beat Schulte

23-8
- at Copenhagen: caught Pohnetal
- at Copenhagen: beat Piel

24-8
- at Copenhagen: beat Pedersen
- at Copenhagen: beat Gillen

30-8
- at Amsterdam: beaten by Schulte

22-9
- at Milan: beat Biagioni
- at Milan: beat Benfenati
- at Milan: beaten by Bevilacqua

1953
25-4
- at Milan: beat Patterson

4-9
- at Milan: beat Patterson

1954
19-4
- at Milan: beaten by Koblet

27-11
- at Milan: beat Bobet

1955
30-6
- at Milan: beat Gillen

23-7
- at Paris: beat Bobet

9-10
- at Milan: beaten by Messina

1958, At the Six-day in Buenos-Aires, Argentina. Coppi with motoring racing legend Juan Manuel Fangio

The 'boys' together; Coppi, Van Steenbergen and Anquetil, Paris 1958

Fausto, Giulia
and Faustino

Nice Airport. Coppi returns with the 'White Lady'

Faustino tries 'Daddies' bike for size!

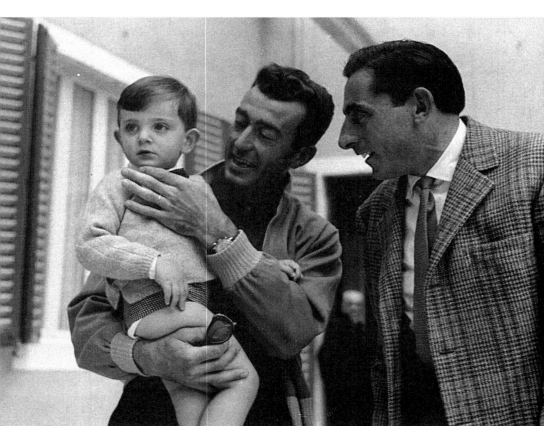

Bobet looking after 'Faustino' while visiting the 'Campionissimo'

'Smile for the camera'. 'Faustino' with mum and Dad at the entrance to the 'Villa Coppi' at Novi-Ligure

Paris-Nice 1958, the rue d'Uzè, young Faustino poses!

ILLUSTRATIONS

*With friends at Tortona. On the right, Carrea and Milan, two of the faithful 'gregari'
that supported the Campionissimo*